SEASONS OF GOLD

JEFF WILSON
SEASONS OF GOLD

with Ron Palenski

Hodder Moa Beckett

Front Cover Photo: Photosport
Back Cover Photo: Studio Microdot
Pages 2-3:   Jeff Wilson celebrates scoring at Carisbrook in the 28-0 demolition of South Africa in 1999.
     Barry Harcourt/Southland Times
Pages 6-7:   Wilson had beaten the Springboks, but what's Anton Oliver doing there?
     Barry Harcourt/Southland Times
Pages 10-11:   Wilson gets outside Tim Horan during the 1997 test against Australia in Christchurch.
     Photosport

ISBN 1-86958-830-4

© 2000 Text — Clifftop Holdings Ltd
The moral rights of the author have been asserted.

Published in 2000 by Hodder Moa Beckett Publishers Ltd
[a member of the Hodder Headline Group],
4 Whetu Place, Mairangi Bay, Auckland

Designed, typeset and produced by Hodder Moa Beckett Publishers Ltd
Film and colour separations by Microdot, Auckland
Printed by Toppan Printing Co. (Hong Kong)

Acknowledgements

I extend my heartfelt thanks to my mother Lynne, to brother Richard and his wife Jo, and to David Howman and Richard Reid — for being there when I needed them.

I thank also my Otago teammates for the memories and the good times over the years.

Thanks also to Ron Palenski for his help with this book.

Dedication

To the memory of Bill – father, friend, mentor,
counsellor, all-round good guy.

Contents

Introduction

It was a rare night, the rarer because it was unscripted and unexpected. The Otago Highlanders were having their final training session for their first match of the 1998 Super 12, two nights distant against the Queensland Reds.

It was at home, at Carisbrook, and the big lights on four towers were on for the first time in earnest. It was a night of little or no meaning for the wider rugby world, just another practice under lights.

The players, having listened to the last pre-training exhortation from their coach, Tony Gilbert, ran out onto the field, stretching as they did, some idly punting or dropkicking the ball toward some random spot.

There were a few spectators. The team management. A camera crew. A couple of reporters. A newspaper photographer. A few fans who had somehow slipped through the players' entrance, the only way in at night.

Someone first raised it diffidently, as if the brain couldn't accept what the eyes were telling it.

"Is that Jeff Wilson out there?"

Someone barely looked and said, "Nah, he's injured. He's out."

But then someone else took up the call. "It is Wilson!"

Indeed it was, the unmistakable fair hair flopping in the night air, the long, loping stride, the head turning this way and that, constantly chatting to his teammates.

Nothing remarkable about Jeff Wilson at a Highlanders training. Yet this training was remarkable. Wilson had been injured, scheduled to miss the first three games of the Super 12 that year because of a thumb injury, a legacy of the All Blacks' tour of Britain and Ireland the year before.

He hadn't been training with the team, instead keeping up his fitness in a lonely regime of gymnasium work, cycling, running and pool sessions.

But now he was back. If not in the team, at least training with them.

His presence sent a murmur round the few people watching. They stood instead of leaned, watched intently instead of idly. The cameraman hefted his camera back on his tripod, the photographer screwed the long lens back in.

The effect on Wilson's teammates was as electric as it was on those watching. The passing seemed snappier, the running sharper, the calling more decisive. There was a spring in the step, the mood was lighter, more confident. "Goldie" was back and, since he was back, all was well with the world.

It was an eerie feeling that night and remains with those who were there. Could one player in the ultimate of team games make such a difference, a difference moreover not in a game, but at practice? Could one player, by his mere presence rather than by deeds, lift those around him?

Yes, one could. If that player was Jeff Wilson. It may have been coincidental that, two nights later, the Highlanders beat the Reds in their opening match. There are many factors that go into the winning or losing of a rugby match, by no means all of them factors on the field of play. Those who were at that final training saw no coincidence at all. Wilson's presence was one of those factors, there was no doubt.

It is a very special sort of player who inspires confidence in those around him, who by his presence and by his deeds can make a noticeable difference. Such a player is Jeff Wilson.

There have been games in which he has played that his team should have lost, but won because of his presence. It's easy to say that of some teams, especially if the player who makes the difference is also the goalkicker. It can be said less often that one single player can not just dominate but sway the outcome of a match.

One example of Wilson's influence was when Otago met Wellington in the National Provincial Championship in 1997. It was Wilson's game. Wellington were the better team, most people afterward acknowledged, and should have won the game. But they didn't. Otago won because of Wilson. When there was a break to be made, he made it; a tackle to be made, he made it; a piece of skill required to keep the ball in Otago's possession, Wilson was the man. Even the Wellington coach, Frank Walker, had to acknowledge the mastery. "We weren't beaten by Otago," he said, "we were beaten by Wilson."

There were other times, other games, right from the first in the early 90s when word spread from Invercargill that a teenager called Wilson was performing prodigious feats and was worth watching. Hadn't he been outstanding in a school match and the *Southland Times* headed its story, "Jeff Wilson 66, James Hargest 6"? A school match yes, but wait until the big time; would he be able to hack it then? the critics asked.

The answer wasn't long in coming. Wilson, Willy the Kid, the Golden Boy, the Golden One, or just Goldie, had skill, talent and competitiveness that belonged to few sports people.

Such players come along but rarely, perhaps once in a generation, perhaps once in the lifetimes of those watching.

He was a cricketer of extreme note too and the question was asked early: Which sport would he choose? It was a question he chose not to answer until an answer was forced upon him and, in the interim, he played both rugby and cricket for New Zealand when he was still a teenager. He became just the second "double All Black" since the Second World War and, in all probability in an age of increased specialisation, the last.

His first impact on the national stage was through cricket, not rugby, his match-winning innings of 44 not out in a one-dayer in Hamilton against Australia bringing forth the repetitive clichés about *Boys' Own*, how one teenager's reality was the dreams of all others.

When he was first chosen for the All Blacks later that year, 1993, coach Laurie Mains wondered about his youth and the risk of exposure of one so young in years and experience to the rigours of international rugby, especially in England, where anyone in a black jersey is fair game. Mains considered not choosing Wilson for the tests, believing that the experience of just touring with the All Blacks would be sufficient grounding. But Mains, in the end, had no choice. It was not so much a question of, "Can I pick Jeff Wilson?" but more, "How can I not pick him?"

Wilson in his first match as an All Black, at Twickenham against a South-West Division team sprinkled with England internationals, was as devastating for New Zealand as he had been for Cargill High School. His play that day set the tone for his tour and it was automatic that he was chosen for his first test, against Scotland, and it was almost inevitable that he had a starring role, scoring three tries and converting the last of them from the touchline with a nonchalant ease.

But all was not golden for Wilson on that tour or for the rest of his rugby career. The following test, against England, exposed Wilson to the harsh realities of international rugby. The All Blacks lost and, as luck would have it, Wilson had had to take over the goalkicking, and he blamed his missed kicks at goal for the loss. It was a humbling lesson. Perhaps for the first time in his young life, Wilson had to confront failure. His teammates said he shouldn't take the blame, the loss wasn't his fault, but Wilson felt that it was. As he slumped, desolate, in the dressing room afterward, one of the players went to comfort him, but Mike Brewer held him back and said: "Let him suffer. It's a lesson for him."

All sports people, the further they climb the ladder to the élite, learn lessons along the way and there was another for Wilson the following year. It was something that Wilson learned not so much about himself, but about the fickleness of the public, how a hero one day can be the villain the next. How the public, frustrated and disappointed, reach out for the most obvious target to assuage their own anger and frustration. It was the 1994 test against Australia in Sydney and it was the match of the George Gregan tackle. How the All Blacks were behind early in the match, got back into it in the second half and how Wilson had the winning of the game clutched in his hands. How he got to the Australian goal-line and how Gregan came from seemingly

15

nowhere to tackle Wilson and jolt the ball forward out of his arms. The public focused on that one decisive moment. Did it marvel that Wilson beat three or four tacklers to get even that far? No, of course not. That's not the way human nature works. What's remembered, and what Wilson is constantly reminded of still, is that he lost the ball in the tackle. The continuing references to that incident are not so much reminders of an assumed Wilson mistake, but of the constant — and sometimes unrealistic — demands by the public for the All Blacks to win every game. Such demands are both a compliment to the enduring excellence of the All Blacks, and a burden to the players.

For every Wilson mistake, they fade away against the overwhelming good that he has brought to the game. There is a sense, even when he may not be playing well by his own high standards or when his team is not playing well, that in a lightning moment he could turn a game around. It could be just a flick of a pass infield, or the leaping for a high ball and turning in midair to deliver down to his support, or it could be a defensive tackle that has the saving of a game written all over it . . . it could be many things.

One of the tricks of the trade that selectors adopt from time to time is not to watch a game for the sake of the game, but to watch one player, to follow his every move, whether the ball is near him or not. Such a study allows selectors to analyse the lines a player runs, to judge his sense of anticipation and his vision of the game, and to get a feel for the player's level of commitment. Such a study of Wilson during a game is illuminating. Even when on the wing and bereft of possession, Wilson somehow contrives to be always involved, to be searching out the action and the options. His peripheral vision, his ability to see what's going on either side of him and even behind him, and his ability to think several moves ahead, take him beyond the ken of most players.

There have been times in Wilson's rugby career when everything seemed to come together at the right place at the right time, either for his own satisfaction or for that of his team. There was the game in Wellington in 1997, and there have been many others like that; there was the epic series in South Africa in 1996 when the All Blacks won there for the first time, there was the NPC final in 1998 when Otago won.

But there have been other times when he and his teams have reached out for the ultimate prize, only to be denied it. This occurred most cruelly at the World Cup in 1995 when the All Blacks were, by common consent, the most complete team there. Whatever the causes, the food poisoning the All Blacks suffered before the cup final against the Springboks ended their hopes and their dreams. This is not to subscribe to any hare-brained theories of being nobbled or of bookmakers in London calling the shots; simply the fact that the All Blacks were ill, Wilson among the worst affected. The All Blacks in 1995 could at least take some comfort in the fact they were a superior team and that they were beaten by factors beyond their control.

Much more hurtful to the players themselves, and to the country as a whole, was the loss four years later in the cup semifinal to France. Theories abounded after that loss as well, theories that had more to do with the supposed "culture" of the team and of élite rugby in general than they did with the actual playing of the game. Wilson was not happy with the selection of the All Black team, but doesn't offer that as an excuse for a loss that many people in New Zealand, some informed, most ill-informed, held to be inexcusable. What it all came down to was what happened out in the middle, that the French for half a game played better and thought smarter than the All Blacks. It was a bitter end to a campaign that had promised so much, a bitter end to Wilson's wish to be a part of an All Black team that won the World Cup.

It may be an appropriate time for a reminder that if it hadn't been for Wilson and his Otago teammate and friend, Josh Kronfeld, the All Blacks may not have got even as close as that to winning the cup; there may not have even been a World Cup. That is not overstating the case. New Zealand rugby had been in turmoil four years before in the face of the raid on New Zealand players by the World Rugby Corporation, a body that had selfish dreams for the future of the game.

Most of the All Blacks, including Wilson and Kronfeld, had signed for the WRC, had indicated their willingness to join the rebel troupe and turn their backs on New Zealand. Had they gone, and make no mistake, they went very close to going, there still would have been a New Zealand Rugby Union and there still would have been All Blacks. But New Zealand would have required a lot longer than four years for the All Blacks to be restored to a level capable of winning the cup (assuming there would still have been a cup to be won). What turned the tide, what caused the WRC ideas to be stillborn, came down to many, varied factors. But in New Zealand, the undoubted catalyst was the decision by Wilson and Kronfeld to spurn the WRC and remain with the New Zealand union. When they signed with New Zealand, the others followed.

Wilson may not like to be remembered grandly as the saviour of All Black rugby, but that in essence is what he and Kronfeld were.

He did not make that decision in isolation or just with Kronfeld. His advisors at the time, and for much of his sporting career, were his father Bill, lawyer David Howman, and the former international cricketer, Richard Reid, who at the time ran Nike's operations in New Zealand. They were the triumvirate that guided Wilson, whose advice he listened to and whom he trusted without reservation. The partnership was a simple one: he did the business on the field, they took care of business off it.

The key figure of the three was Bill, a jovial, no-nonsense Southlander who was a more than handy cricketer and footballer himself and who saw earlier than anyone that his youngest son had special sporting gifts.

Bill's death from a heart attack late in 1998 was a shattering blow to

Barry Harcourt/Southland Times

Father and son at Carisbrook before Jeff's first one-dayer for New Zealand.

Wilson. Any son grieves the loss of his father sorely. Bill was more than "just" a father. He was also friend, mentor, counsellor, business manager, any number of titles. Bill was the first person to whom Wilson would turn — for advice, for encouragement, for a chat. The younger Wilson would listen to the older, take heed of what he was saying.

The relationship between the two was special, even more special because Wilson was the superstar. It is one of the side-effects of stardom in sport, as in most other spheres of activity, that the person at the centre of attention finds there are a decreasing number of people he can trust or who he can take seriously; sycophants surround the stars like moths around a light bulb.

If Bill felt Wilson had not played well or had made some dumb move in a game or elsewhere, he would tell him. Suddenly, without Bill, Wilson did not have access to the same honesty of purpose. Wilson knew that when he came off the field, he would get an honest, frank appraisal from his father. But without his father, he was being told by sycophants what they thought he might want to hear. The honesty was missing.

Wilson's mother, Lynne, knowing what was missing, kept in contact as much as she could but she did not have the same insights that Bill had had.

For the first time in Wilson's sporting career, some of the joy, some of the zest for sport, was missing.

The sense of loss Wilson felt was there for all to see, if those doing the looking knew what to look for. From the first match of the 1999 Super 12, Wilson carried out on to the ground a small handful of sand, which he sprinkled on to the turf before taking up his position. He did this every match, his personal acknowledgement to Bill. It was a poignant gesture. It went unremarked and, largely, unnoticed, which was the way Wilson wanted it.

In memoriam.

19

Until Bill died, Wilson's career remained full of hope. Without Bill, it was apparent that the end of the remarkable career was closer than it had been.

There are other pressures on high-profile sports people that those on the outside can barely imagine and none comes more high profile in New Zealand than the All Blacks. The constant attention, the demands on time for all manner of activities, many of which are not directly related to the playing of the game, have the effect of wearing a player down. A few thrive on such attention, but most don't. Wilson didn't. He accepted that his status — his job — carried with it certain obligations and disadvantages, and he fulfilled these when he had to, without necessarily enjoying them. He was careful about drawing the line between the public Jeff Wilson and the private, arguing with validity that some aspects of life were his to know about, and no one else.

For all the fame, and for all the wealth that his sporting talent has brought, Wilson remains pretty much as he always was. An enthusiast for sport and for life in general, but someone who also values his times alone and who, sometimes, prefers to be alone. As the years of rugby in a goldfish bowl accumulated, the time to return to being Jeff Wilson, private person, edged closer. Perhaps a return to cricket, perhaps something else. But whatever it is, he knows that he will never be "ordinary" because whatever he does in the future, he will forever be known for his extraordinary deeds on the sporting field.

And memories will remain with those of us who were privileged to see him and his palatine skills, memories like these contained in a poem published in Gisborne, written by Robin Thurston of Puha:

Day is telecast through night,
The future signals past time.
Woken eyes (from local grind)
Get pictures of a rugby ground
Somewhere north of England.
One boy, to all boys becomes
Ourselves, the ball in our own hands,
Sidestepping his way past Scotland,
Slipping through life like a knife for us,
All gold, in his All Black jersey
. . . And sitting bolt upright in bed
Half a grateful nation cheers
As half a world away he tears
Towards a tryline.
Tears spring from our blinding speed . . .

Ron Palenski, Dunedin, 2000

1. Living for weekends

Growing up in Invercargill, life seemed to be one long weekend of sport. It wasn't of course, it just seemed that way, especially when looking back on it now. Even the weekdays at school had an aspect of the weekend about them because sport was a big part of my early life, just as it has continued to be.

Every weekend seemed to revolve around sport from when I was just past the toddler stage, going to rugby or cricket with my father Bill and older brother Richard, or going to the tennis courts with my mother, Lynne, who had been good enough to play for Otago and Southland and had been in an Otago team that won the Nunneley Casket. Dad had played cricket for Southland and club rugby in both Dunedin and Invercargill and his brother John had also been a rugby player and played cricket for Otago and Southland. We were a sports-mad family but not, I suspect, all that different to a lot of other New Zealand families.

Cricket was the ruling passion and the hub was the Appleby Cricket Club, a sort of home away from home both then and now. When Dad was playing, I'd sometimes wander out into the middle in my earlier days but it didn't take too long to learn my place. If Mum was away playing tennis, there were always other players' wives to keep an eye on me, and Richard, being four years older than me, was also burdened with the responsibility that big brothers bear. I soon learned where I could and couldn't go and what I could do and what I couldn't get away with.

I also had a responsibility, shared with Richard, at the end of each day to get our father home. He'd be in the clubhouse doing whatever it was the big people did after a hot day in the field and when the phone went with Mum inquiring about progress, Richard or I always knew we had to say, "Yep, we're just on the way." For such support, we usually received another raspberry or lemonade until the next phone call.

It was just a matter of time and size until I started playing. I was seven when I first started going to cricket practice and didn't want for any coaching because Dad and Uncle John were both well versed in the game and were willing and enthusiastic teachers. I began more as a batsman but it wasn't

The peaceful sleep of an eight-year-old, with my first rugby trophy.

long before I was bowling as well and, given that Dad and Uncle John were both medium-fast bowlers and that Appleby always seemed to have quick bowlers, it was natural that I followed suit. In my youthful enthusiasm, I just bowled as fast as I could. I had a terrible action. I used to sling it down in the shortest possible time. My action certainly didn't belong to any textbook but it seemed to be effective. I remember playing for Newfield Primary one day and a boy to whom I'd been bowling went and complained to the headmaster, Alistair Tait — better known as "Spud" Tait, Southland rugby player and coach — with words along these lines: "Please sir, Jeffrey Wilson is bowling too fast again!"

My batting wasn't all that refined either. My approach to batting was pretty much the same as to bowling and I tried to hit every ball out of the ground. It was only later that Billy Ibadulla, the Otago cricket coach who has been such an influence on so many cricketers from the south, including Glenn Turner, took me aside and taught me some of the finer points of batting. He would only allow me to play backward and forward defensive shots, insisting I should have a background of solid technique before lashing out. Patience, though, was seldom a virtue. Far more satisfying to hit a six than to see the ball dribble back down the pitch to the bowler.

I was involved in athletics in a big way at the same time and I was bigger and quicker than most of the kids I was competing against. I think the reason for that, and this applied in cricket too, was that the cutoff date for birthdates

A gold medal at the Colgate Games in Christchurch in 1984.

when determining ages for teams was then 1 October and because I was born in later October — 24 October 1973, to be precise — I had a height and weight advantage over other kids in the same age group.

I suspect Mum introduced me to athletics because she had to drop me off somewhere while she played tennis. There was no such thing as specialising then and I had a go at most events, discovering that I was best at the long jump and shot put, which is a pretty weird combination when you come to think of it. I ran in the sprints as well but seldom beyond 200 metres. Events such as the 400 or 800 metres were much too far for me. I liked my sports to be explosive. Get in there and do it and get it over with: hitting a six, bowling fast, sprints, shot put, long jump — all instant action. None of this long, patient stuff with strategies and tactics for me.

While I enjoyed athletics, my career in it was brief. There just wasn't time to do everything and, not for the first time, I had to make a choice between sports and cricket won. But athletics gave me my first overseas trip and my first international competition — at the ripe old age of 10 when I competed for New Zealand in the shot put at a Pan Pacific primary schools tournament in Melbourne. The venue was one with which I would much later become better acquainted, the Melbourne Cricket Ground. I hardly distinguished myself there as a shot putter, though, finishing somewhere in the middle of the field.

I'd had some athletics success locally, winning three titles at the Otago-Southland primary schools championships in Oamaru one year. I got a flyer in the 100 metres final, so much of a flyer it must have been bordering on a break, and won that, and also won the shot put. I was second in the long jump after straining a groin muscle. I was still picked for the South Island championships in Christchurch where Nick Broughton, a later rugby colleague, beat me in the shot but I was able to win the long jump with just one jump, the groin preventing me from doing any more. But the one was enough.

It was around this time that I also took up basketball, playing on Friday nights and not, I think, accompanied by great enthusiasm from Dad. But I loved it. It's a great game and one to which I'm still addicted. I think what drew me to basketball was the speed and the non-stop action, much more than any other game. I wasn't much of a dribbler and I still can't shoot, though I try, but I was a reasonably good defensive player. It was through basketball that I met Tab Baldwin, a man with whom I've remained in close contact and one of the best coaches in New Zealand. He'd coached the Nuggets in Dunedin for a while and he was coaching in Invercargill, working out of the YMCA. He had me in the Southland under 18 team and we thought we were pretty special when we went to the South Island tournament but in reality we were only the third or fourth best team there.

But thanks to Tab's coaching and our belief in ourselves, we ended up winning. That was my big moment in basketball, though I still follow the sport closely — in fact I probably watch more basketball on television than I do rugby. Guys like Michael Jordan, Magic Johnson and Larry Bird were just such amazing athletes, examples for anyone in any sport. My obsession with basketball continues and I practise my shooting with a hoop at home every chance I get. You just never know.

Tab, who had impressed upon me the need to get the fundamentals right before anything else, wanted me to continue in basketball and I was fairly keen, but Dad wasn't. My father was pretty sharp and knew sport inside out and he just didn't see a future for me in basketball, whereas rugby and cricket were entirely different matters. When it became apparent that I might have some success in sport, he and Mum used to joke about Dad carrying my bags to Lord's or The Oval or somewhere.

Growing up is a kaleidoscope of memories of fun and sport interspersed with schoolwork. I didn't neglect the latter, and my parents ensured that I didn't and that schoolwork came before sport, but I can't say I ever enjoyed it. My marks were always good enough without being brilliant, though I must say I was good at mathematics — that was because I played sport and maths is one of the few school subjects that have a direct relationship to sport! I didn't get involved in any of the extra activities at school such as music. I'm no musician, as anyone who has heard me sing can testify, but it's a little-known fact that I once recorded a song. I'm one of the chorus on the recording of the Highlanders song but it will take a very acute ear to pick my voice out. I'm quite happy to leave that sort of stuff to Josh.

The Wilson family home was no different I suppose to many others, especially when the only children were boys. Richard and I would play just

The family home in Invercargill . . . a house of happy memories.

about every game imaginable outside or in the wide hallway, diminishing the value of the carpet and wrecking a few planks. After cricket or golf sessions at home, we'd rush around tidying up and replacing divots so we had suitably innocent airs when Mum and Dad got home from work. But I don't think they were ever fooled. They always seemed to know what we'd been up to. The only window we ever broke was through playing soccer in the street. We played sport rather than followed it. We were never autograph seekers at rugby or cricket, we never avidly followed test matches on the radio or on television. Even when I was at Tweedsmuir Intermediate and chosen to be a ball boy at a rugby World Cup game in Invercargill, I didn't take all that much interest in the game and didn't try to get players' autographs afterward.

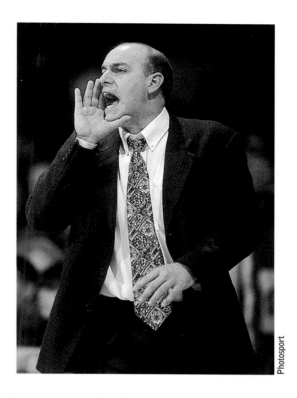

Photosport

Tab Baldwin, basketball coach and close friend.

My cricket took off long before my rugby did, probably because it's more feasible in cricket for younger, less developed kids to play against adults in cricket than it is in rugby. I had no problem playing senior cricket at the age of 14, but I would have had a great deal of problems trying to play senior rugby at that age, especially if some of the grizzled old guys in front rows decided to teach the young pup a few lessons. My cricket also developed earlier because I was much more interested in it than I was in rugby.

People outside my family, the Appleby club and immediate friends started to take notice when I went to a South Island primary schools tournament in Christchurch. I bowled non-stop from one end — remember this was at an age when tiredness is something that happens to someone else — and opponents in one game refused to shake hands afterward because they reckoned I was intimidating their batsmen. In another game, I'd been taken off and was fielding in the covers and feeling a bit grumpy when a chance was hit to me. I didn't see it properly and it hit me in the nose. I got pretty fired up and almost demanded to be given another bowl and I just went nuts. I took 10–27 which I was told broke a record set by Richard Hadlee. I was snarling and talking and yelling and generally being obnoxious. It wouldn't have been tolerated for anyone over 18. But it was successful. I've always had a competitive nature and what's the point of playing sport if you're not going to be competitive, if you're not going to give 100 per cent every time you play? Settling for anything less is just settling for the mediocre and that's not what sport should be about.

My bowling action then was still fairly wild and uncontrolled and, ironically, it was a rugby injury that tempered my bowling. I'd broken a wrist playing in the inter-island under 16 match in Wellington — my first experience of Athletic Park — about a month before the cricket season and I'd also been having trouble with my back. So I decided to change my bowling action and I got hold of a video of Richard Hadlee and decided to bowl just like him. This was when he had adopted his short run. I copied everything he did and the whole time I was practising I was saying to myself, "I'm Hadlee, I'm Hadlee."

By this time, rugby was becoming a more important part of my life though cricket remained the main passion. I'd started playing at halfback because I had a reasonable pass off both hands and halfback was a position guaranteed to get hold of the ball, and that was exactly what I wanted. I was at halfback through primary and intermediate school and moved to first five-eighth when I started at Cargill High School because I'd grown too big to be a halfback. George Hau, who had chosen me for the Southland under 58 kg team a couple of years before, rang me and asked if I'd considered playing fullback. I hadn't and in fact I'd even considered not playing rugby that year, 1988, because I was conscious that a rugby injury had ended Uncle John's career as a cricketer and I didn't want that to happen to me. But George was persuasive and I found myself as fullback in the Southland under 16 team at the South Island tournament in Blenheim and, subsequently, chosen for the South Island to play the North, the match in which I broke my wrist.

He had me back the following year when I again made the South Island team and in 1990 I made the national under 17 team, thanks to a lucky break. Todd Miller, then in Northland, was the first choice as fullback for the team's tour of Australia but because there were Sunday matches and he was a Mormon, he had to make himself unavailable. That led to me being chosen and I played in all five games. At this stage, I hadn't even played for the Cargill High School First XV though that wasn't long in coming.

One match in 1992 for the school against the James Hargest First XV gave me more national publicity than I ever needed or wanted. In the equivalent match the previous year, I'd been caught on the bottom of a ruck and got gashed in the head. There was talk about it being deliberate to get

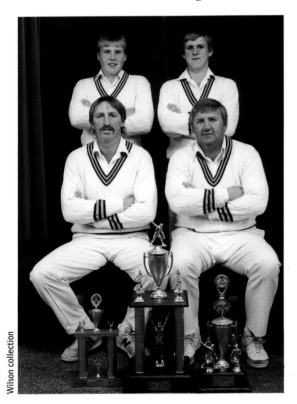

Wilson collection

A family affair . . . Uncle John (left) and Dad in front and Richard and I with the Appleby senior cricket team's trophies in 1988.

me out of the game, but I don't know about that. All I knew was that we were after revenge the next year and we declared total war on James Hargest. It wasn't war, it was a massacre. We won 102-6 and I scored nine tries and kicked 16 conversions for 66 points,

How the Southland Times **saw the massacre.**

which grabbed a bit of media attention, including television cameras showing up at school the next day. The focus was on me because of the scoring, but really the whole team played a blinder — as any team has to in order to reach a score like that. It was a very satisfying win after what had gone on the year before.

That same year, I was in the national secondary schools team that went to Australia and we routed the Aussies in the one "test". The 31-8 win in Sydney was particularly satisfying for me because it was one of those games that happen all too rarely when you achieve what you set out to do and everything goes right. You take the high ball, you find touch, you are never caught out of position, you make your tackles, you hit the line at precisely the right times and you kick well — it was just one of those games. We were also a pretty good team with guys in it that I've continued playing with either with Otago or the All Blacks, such as Daryl Gibson, Jeremy Stanley, Todd Miller, Carlos Spencer, Isitolo Maka, Chresten Davis, Royce Willis and Carl Hoeft. And oh yes, there was a big bloke called Jonah Lomu at No 8.

Spot the future All Blacks. The 1992 secondary schools team that beat Australia and Ireland. Ten of us are there somewhere – Royce Willis, Chresten Davis, Jonah Lomu, Carlos Spencer, Isitolo Maka, Jeremy Stanley, Carl Hoeft, Daryl Gibson, Todd Miller and me.

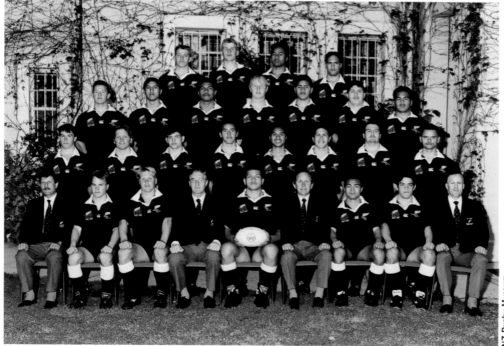

NZ Rugby Museum

By then, I'd already played for Southland, first at fullback and then on the wing because of the presence of Simon Forrest at fullback. Being chosen for Southland was a direct result of me having to take a half-day off school to play for Invercargill Metropolitan against Otago Country. That was more or less a trial for the Southland team and I guess I did enough in our 33-19 win to make the step up. I was lucky because it was another one of those games in which everything seemed to go right. It could so easily have gone the other way, especially for a schoolboy confronting the hard, experienced men for the first time. At that stage, I had matured enough to be able to handle such games physically.

Ready to pounce in my first first-class match, for Southland against Canterbury in 1992.

Southland Times

Through all this fairly rapid rugby development, I was still a cricketer and things were happening there too and it was apparent that the day was not far off when I would have to make a choice, but I put that off for as long as I could. I'd been playing for Southland in the U-Bix Cup since I was 15, had played for the New Zealand Youth team for three years, including a tour of India that was utterly unmemorable, and had made my début for Otago in both the Shell Cup and the Shell Trophy. And not forgetting playing for Appleby, for whom I was taking wickets regularly and in one memorable match, Dad, Richard and I took all 10 wickets between us.

I'd also had the great benefit of coaching from Dennis Lillee and Richard Hadlee, each of whom taught me the value of control. But while I was getting good advice from them, probably the person I listened to most was Dad because he was a good cricketer and had such a fine sporting brain. He understood sport as well as anyone I know, better than most, and of course he understood me better than anyone.

But there were lessons on the field too. In every game you play, no matter what the game is, you learn something new or there's something you see or hear that you file away for future reference. This may apply more in cricket than in rugby because there are so many more variables — the state of the wicket or the weather, the length of the match, the differing qualities of opponents you're batting or bowling against. In cricket you can score 100 and in the overall scheme of the game it may not mean much, but then you could score 20 or 30 that would be absolutely crucial to your side. When bowling, you may not take wickets but you know you've done your job from one end by containing the batsmen. Then again, you may get carted around the park in one over. That happened to me in the first Shell Cup game I played, against Auckland at Alexandra. After nine overs I had one for 32 which wasn't great, but wasn't bad either. Then Ian Smith took 22 off my last over, which didn't do much for my figures or for my confidence. But that's the way you learn in top-class sport. If we could repeat those exact circumstances, me bowling a final over to him, I'd bowl it a lot differently next time. But then, he might play me differently too.

That's the great beauty of sport. It's using the physical skills you've practised against people who are very skilful in their own right, and complementing the physical with the mental, trying to think quicker and smarter than your opponent.

In cricket as a bowler, you learn and remember which batsmen are most susceptible to which balls, or as a batsman you learn to expect what types of deliveries you're going to get from whom. In rugby, you know that some players can't make an outside break or can step off only one foot, or you know that a kicker is weaker with one foot than another. The more you play, the more you file away into your own memory bank, to be recalled in that

Barry Harcourt/Southland Times

In the Shell Cup final against Canterbury in 1993 – J W Wilson c Germon b Owens 5.

split second when you have to decide what to do. Sport is a constant challenge and when it's not, it's time to find something else to do.

In the early 90s, my father and a few other people in Invercargill with vision and an understanding of sport helped me put together a CV. It was aimed primarily at helping to raise funds to send me on various sports trips because too often I had had to turn to my parents or my maternal grandmother in Dunedin, Grace Robertson, for help. An active sporting life for young people is all very well, but it can be an expensive business until selection in teams which pay the bills can be attained. In this CV, I wrote my philosophy in which I said commitment was the key to my life and that through this, success could be attained. "My dedication to my sport, whether it be rugby or cricket, is wholly through the love of the game, the pressure of competition and the passion to succeed."

Years later, though rugby has made me moderately wealthy, I don't see any reason to change that view.

2. The big wide world

Sometimes things happen in someone's life that become just part of a mass of influential factors. There are things you know happened, but while you might be able to remember the broad impact, the details are lost and gone forever. Anyone who's tried to put their life story down on paper will know the feeling well. "Well yes, such and such happened but I can't for the life of me remember anything about it." But there are other moments in time that remain with you always, as if they happened just the day before.

Detective Gordon Hunter lays down the law at halftime.

Such an occasion was the day a policeman came to the Wilson home in Invercargill.

A knock on the door. I answered.

"G'day lad," the apparition said, "are your parents at home?"

In some households, I suppose, such a visitation would produce that sick, sinking feeling in the stomach. What have I done? Who saw me do it? Oh God, I'm in trouble now.

But this visit had nothing to do with a breach of the law and I wasn't about to be asked something along the lines of, "And where were you lad, on the night of the 24th?"

The visitor was Gordon Hunter, detective. Fortunately for me, he was also Gordon Hunter, coach of the Otago rugby team.

But it still came as something of a surprise to see this big strapping bloke at the door, bushy eyebrows overhanging one eye staring down at me. (In case there's some New Zealander who's been in isolation for 10 years, Gordon lost an eye in an accident in the garden. It would be a much better story if he'd lost it in the valiant pursuit of some hardened criminal, sacrificing half his sight to create a better world for the rest of us. But such is life. It has the dramatic and the prosaic.)

31

Gordon wasn't there to see me. Other than my acting the host and letting him in, I may as well not have been there. He was with Mum and Dad for about an hour, sitting in the lounge and chatting to them. I was there, perched on a chair listening to every word, but none of Gordy's words was directed at me. As far as he was concerned, I could have been nothing more than a picture on the wall. I was about as noisy as one as well.

That was toward the end of 1992 when I'd already played rugby for Southland and the purpose of Gordy's visit was to find out something about me and, I think, to assure my parents that I'd be in good hands by being a member of the wide Otago family. I'd already been accepted to go to the College of Education in Dunedin — teachers' college as most still call it — and Gordy knew that. He didn't talk about the possibility of my playing for Otago, merely about the community spirit that exists in Otago rugby and how the players, the management and administration all form a happy relationship. He talked about some of the Otago players, guys such as Jamie Joseph, Arran Pene, Stu Forster and John Timu, and to me, it all sounded a bit of a distant dream to be playing on the same side as them. I knew the names of course, but I wasn't much of a rugby follower because my life revolved so much around doing rather than watching.

This is the point at which I should say that Gordon Hunter's visit to our house in Invercargill changed my life forever, a watershed moment in the career of a young sportsman wondering where he was headed. But it wasn't like that at all. I was headed for Dunedin anyway and he knew that. It was, I suppose, a getting-to-know-you sort of visit.

The interview process to get into the College of Education involved meeting a panel of, from memory, four people and explaining why I wanted to be a teacher and them asking me an endless number of questions about my education and attitude. It all seemed to go pretty well because I was accepted, but I learned several years later that some of the panel had been sceptical before the interview. They had evidently read about me before I made my appearance and had wondered if I wasn't just some sports jock wanting to go to college to fill in time between rugby and cricket and practising for both. Somehow, during the interview and assessment, I was able to convince them I would be a worthy addition to their student roll and I ended up with a pass mark well above the average. One of the panel was Peter Sinclair, who I later learned had played senior club rugby in Invercargill, and who was a close friend of Tony Gilbert. Several years on, he had a critical role with the Otago Highlanders and the Otago NPC team.

Teaching and I were destined not to meet, however. Within a couple of days of starting at college, my grandmother Grace Robertson, with whom I lived in Dunedin, asked me when I got home one day if I'd heard the news.

"What news?" I asked.

"You're in the New Zealand cricket team," she said as she hugged me.

I had to phone Dad in Invercargill and ask him to send my gear back up. Cricket then had been consigned to the back of my mind. I'd had a reasonable season in Shell Cup and Shell Trophy, but nothing spectacular, and getting into the New Zealand team had not seemed to me to be even a distant prospect. I hadn't played a one-day game since the cup final at Carisbrook a month before, in which we'd been beaten by Canterbury by 14 runs, and hadn't played any sort of cricket since the Shell Trophy final a couple of weeks earlier, when we'd been beaten by Northern Districts in a rain-affected match in Hamilton.

So here I was, thrust into the big time with the likes of Martin Crowe, Andrew Jones, Dipak Patel, Danny Morrison and others, guys who had been around the national cricket scene for years and heroes of the World Cup efforts the year before. I knew some of them through playing first-class and one-day cricket but only to nod to and say hello. Being in the same team as them and playing international cricket was altogether something much different.

Wilson collection

My grandmother, Grace Robertson, joins in the publicity after I'd been selected for the New Zealand cricket team.

And if the guys I was playing with were big names, those I was playing against were even bigger. The Aussies were captained by Allan Border and they had guys such as David Boon, Dean Jones, Merv Hughes, the two Waughs, cricketing names which to me were television figures on a level several above me.

I thought I'd be there just for a bit of indoctrination, practising with them and sharing the same dressing room but not actually playing. Selectors do that sort of thing sometimes, pick someone just to give them a taste of the off-field atmosphere of international sport. So it was a bit of a surprise on the morning of the first one-day international when Warren Lees, the coach, told me that he'd left out Chris Pringle and Chris Harris and that I would be playing.

I didn't have time to get nervous or even to think too much about the size of the occasion for me because Border won the toss and they batted. That put me in the firing line immediately and as luck would have it, Border and their coach, Bob Simpson, used the game to try out a new opening partnership of Mark Waugh and Mark Taylor. Unfortunately for us, it worked. Morrison and I opened the bowling and there's not much to be said

beyond the fact they put on 95 off 138 balls. We were rarely in the game and were beaten by 129 runs and my début in international cricket, I thought, might also be my departure from international cricket. I had a pretty poor start. I took one for 58 off my 10 overs (Damien Martin became my first international wicket) and was bowled for a fourth-ball duck by Paul Reiffel. So much for the golden boy!

Not surprisingly, I was stood down from the next match in Christchurch which remains notable in New Zealand one-day history only for the fact it was the first to be played over two days after rain had disrupted the first. We lost that one by a wicket and I was brought back in for another chance, in the third match of the series in Wellington. We were much better there, mainly thanks to 91 from Martin Crowe and a typical effort from Gavin Larsen, who took three for 17 off his 10 overs. Larsen was the type of bowler the Aussies regarded as fairly innocuous and therefore they went after him, figuring his end was where the runs would come. But as Larsen so often proved, he is underestimated at the batsman's peril and to the batsman's embarrassment. Although I wasn't one of the great contributors, I felt a little better about my own performance because I scored 15 at a valuable time for New Zealand, though it was a very scratchy 15, and was able to get the wickets of David Boon and Shane Warne. We won by 88 runs, one of the more sizeable New Zealand victories over Australia in one-day internationals, and the old decree that a winning team is never changed got me through to Hamilton.

What a magical day that was, not that I had much to do with the first half of it. The Aussies batted first and I bowled like a bit of a pillock, conceding 20 runs in three overs before Crowe had had enough and he did not beckon to me again. That was when Mark Waugh and Dean Jones were belting the ball all over the place, putting on 143 runs for the second wicket with Waugh getting his first century in a one-dayer. The Australian total of 247 wasn't huge, but it was a respectable score and we knew we'd have to bat better than we had been doing if we were to win. New Zealand cricket once again had Martin Crowe to thank. He batted like a messiah for his 91 off just 118 balls and the Aussies were lucky they were able to run him out. The way he was batting, they wouldn't have got him out any other way. Two innings, two scores of 91 for Crowe. No wonder the Aussies were happy to see the back of him. So often disparaging of New Zealand cricket, the Aussies granted Crowe a grudging respect.

Crowe's batting in that series was all the more remarkable because he was badly affected by the chronic knee injury that eventually ended his career. His range of movement was limited and he must have been in excruciating pain at times. But he batted like a dream, the type of batsman to whom you could point and say, "There's the finest example of technique

Keeping an eye on one through the covers.

With Steve Waugh dispatched to the boundary in Hamilton, it's time to celebrate.

Photosport

and application that you will ever see."

Crowe had set the match up nicely from a spectator point of view because there's nothing worse for the crowd than a one-dayer with a predictable end. Us guys in the middle, though, would have been happier to have played the Aussies out of it much earlier.

I went to the wicket when we were six down; we needed 76 to win and there were only 10 overs left — an asking rate of 7.6 against some of the finest bowlers in the world, Merv Hughes, Tony Dodemaide, Paul Reiffel, Tim May and the two Waughs.

Tony Blain was there waiting for me when I arrived. "No one expects us to win," he told me, "so just stay here as long as you can and enjoy it."

Blain was always a joy to play with because he was such an exuberant character that nothing ever seemed insurmountable or too much trouble. Stack the odds up against him and he'd have fun reducing them. His words to me in Hamilton were just what I wanted to hear. We had to attack and as long as we did it sensibly, we could win the game. We certainly couldn't win by being defensive and cautious so it was a matter of just trying. If we succeeded, fine. If we failed, at least we tried.

Blain was out soon after and Dipak Patel came to join me with a message from Warren Lees, saying "Keep cool". Easy for him to say! I knew what he meant, though: not to let the Aussies rattle me and upset my concentration. I also knew I had to keep the adrenalin going and Dipak and I encouraged each other between overs, just reminding ourselves of the need to get bat on ball.

Patel was run out and Gavin Larsen joined me. Five overs to go, 37 to get. Not impossible, not improbable, but not a cakewalk either. If anything, the Aussies had it slightly over us at that stage. With four overs to go, we still needed 32. With three, we needed 25. It was knife-edge stuff and we needed a big hit to give us something of a cushion, something to bring the pendulum back our way.

Steve Waugh tossed one up. I saw it early and drove. I didn't feel as if I hit it all that hard, it wasn't as if I was trying to knock the cover off the ball. It was just that the timing was right. The ball soared over the long-on boundary for six and I knew when the umpire's arms went up that the match would be ours. The spell had been broken. I think the Aussies sensed it then too. You can tell what your opponents are thinking. The looks on their faces, the attitudes of their heads, hands on the hips, shoulders slump a bit. That six got to them.

With two overs to go, we needed 14 and I was confident by then we'd get them. Gavin Larsen was playing intelligently at the other end and the Aussies were starting to look a bit rattled. It was just a matter of keeping our heads.

Two runs needed and three balls to go, Border brought the field up. Steve Waugh strayed a little from his line, I glanced the ball and turned to see where it had gone. It was heading for the boundary. Victory! I remember punching the air and running for the pavilion to escape the hordes of kids who ran onto the field. It was only later that I realised I'd scored 44 off just 28 balls.

I suppose that innings, or rather the end of it, became something of a defining moment in my life. It was the old *Boy's Own* stuff although this time I wasn't hitting the winning shot in the backyard or in the hallway at home,

Up with the big Aussie names . . . Mark Taylor backs up as I bowl.

Photosport

37

Time to celebrate with Chris Harris and Gavin Larsen.

Photosport

but for New Zealand with "Wilson" emblazoned across my back. It's what kids, including me, dream about. Had I got another scratchy 15 or something in that game, perhaps the fact I'd played cricket for New Zealand would have faded in people's memories, just a little footnote in the rugby histories. But the role I was forced by circumstances into playing elevated me in the public's consciousness.

The most important thing for me, though, was that I felt I had proved myself to myself, that I had earned some respect in New Zealand, and I had shown the Aussies that I could be as competitive as them. I think this showed in the last game, in Auckland, when the Aussies started getting a bit lippy toward me, just a bit of sledging. They'd more or less ignored me previously and I think the fact they gave me a bit of abuse in Auckland was their way of showing that they had noticed me, that I had earned their respect.

I was still on a Hamilton high in Auckland and in my youthful enthusiasm thought all I had to do was show up and it would happen again. I thought that this was just the beginning of a wonderful career, but as it turned out, it was the end. I got 21 in Auckland but didn't bowl all that well and, to make matters worse, we lost.

Not for the first time, and certainly not for the last, I learned that sport can be kind one day and cuttingly cruel the next.

I had another experience in Auckland that was new to me. When I went into bat, we were in fairly major trouble at 139/6 with all the main batsmen already gone. It was clear the big crowd was expecting, even demanding, something of a Hamilton repeat. To my surprise, and I must confess, to my delight, they rose as I walked out and chanted, "Wil-son, Wil-son" . . . this was pretty heady stuff for a 19-year-old. The Eden Park crowd that once chanted "Had-lee, Had-lee" had now cottoned on to a callow youth from Invercargill. Though I got three boundaries in my 21, the fairytale didn't continue.

Among the videos at the family home in Invercargill is one we've called *Hamilton 3*. It may sound immodest or even arrogant to say that I have such a video, even worse to say that I still watch it occasionally. But it's one that the family and I have liked to watch every so often, just as something good to look back on.

It was the end of March when the cricket was all over and I had to get in shape for rugby fairly rapidly because I'd been chosen at the end of 1992 in the New Zealand Divisional team (chosen from the second and third divisions) for a short internal tour in April. So it was back to Dunedin and a couple of club games for Harbour and why I played there was a story in itself. There was plenty of talk that Harbour, one of the newest and least fashionable clubs in Dunedin, must have found plenty of money somewhere to attract me. The truth was, and what an irony it was, that Harbour was the only club that didn't offer me anything.

When I was in Invercargill and the word got around that I was moving to Dunedin, I received some ridiculous offers from Dunedin clubs — houses, cars, jobs at which I wasn't expected to work, all the inducements and blandishments that were then a part of club rugby. There was a fair bit of speculation around that I was going to Southern and I had a meeting with one of its stalwarts, Eion Willis (whose son Tom I was later to play with for the Highlanders and Otago).

But the club that impressed me most was Harbour and I don't think I'd even heard of them. I still thought then of Ravensbourne and Port Chalmers, the two clubs that had merged to form Harbour. But Jack Medder from Harbour rang me and just suggested that I play for them because they wanted me to. No cars, no houses, no jobs, no money, no offers of any kind.

The simple love of the game was my kind of offer and so a Harbour boy I became — and remain.

I had been chosen as a fullback in the Divisional team and the other fullback in the squad was Sam Doyle, a player of promise from Manawatu. The tour was only of three matches and I was among the reserves for each of them, a spectator against King Country and Hawke's Bay, until I finally got a run against Wellington.

The coach was Earle Kirton, who that year was also the assistant All Black coach, and I think his intention for me was that I should just soak up the atmosphere of a rugby tour and otherwise stay in the background while

39

the big boys played. I didn't know it at the time, though he may have had an inkling, but three other members of that Divisional team, Paul Henderson, who was the captain, Marty Berry and Lee Stensness, were to be my teammates again later in the year when the All Blacks went to England and Scotland.

Kirton must have liked something about the way I sat on the bench because the All Black trial teams were chosen shortly after the Divisional tour and, to my surprise, and by the sound of things the surprise of a few people around the country, I was included at fullback for one of the teams in the early trial. There was a bit of media comment that I had been given a trial without having played for Otago (even if I'd been wanted, I couldn't have because the one-day cricket and the Divisional tour clashed with Otago's first few games) but when you're a sensitive 19-year-old, it sounded as if the whole country was complaining.

I wasn't complaining, although I certainly didn't think I had a show of doing anything beyond playing in the trial. There were so many great players there that I was just an anonymous appendage. I'd only been chosen for the Possibles in the early trial and felt that I was there just to make up the numbers. The fullback in the Probables was Shane Howarth from Auckland, who had vastly more first-class experience than I had, and the two in the late trial were John Timu and Sam Doyle. The three selectors, Laurie Mains, Earle Kirton and Peter Thorburn, wouldn't have wanted to look at my goalkicking either because in my team — or rather, the team captained by Zinzan Brooke in which I had been placed — was Grant Fox. I roomed with Fox for the three or four nights we were in Rotorua and it was a learning experience just rubbing shoulders and sharing a room with such a consummate professional as him. I don't recall him sitting me down and saying something like, "Listen kid, this is what you've got to do"; it was more his example that I was able to watch and learn from.

The trial became even more meaningless when on the day of the matches it poured all day. The International Stadium field was almost awash and it was one of those games that seem designed for forward play and in which backs are at risk of hypothermia. My memories of it are not vivid — I recall being stepped by Shane Howarth and that's about all. I did have a couple of runs with the ball before being swamped by tacklers. It was not an auspicious beginning at that level and if anyone had said that night, when the rain continued to fall, that Jeff Wilson would be an All Black by the end of the year, they would have been certified and taken away by attendants in white coats.

As people were quick to point out, I hadn't even played for Otago at that stage. I wondered if I would too because Otago had plenty of talent from which to choose for the outside backs with guys such as Greg Cooper and

A wet, forgettable day in the early All Black trial in Rotorua in 1993.

40

John Timu vying for fullback and Paul Cooke, André Bell and Jason Wright angling for the wing places. Timu was at fullback and Bell and Wright on the wings for the first few games but I played well enough in a couple of club games, especially in one against Southern, to get added to the Otago squad and I made my début at fullback in Timaru against South Canterbury. With all due respect to Kevin Gloag, who was South Canterbury's coach at the time and now coaches Otago and is assistant coach of the Highlanders, South Canterbury were not a great threat to Otago and we won quite comfortably. It wasn't one of my better games but I felt I did sufficiently well to justify my place.

Gordon Hunter must have thought I did enough because though I missed the next two games (including a win against the British Isles) I became more or less a regular member of the team (as much as any players can consider themselves regular, given the vagaries of form and the caprices of selectors). By the time the National Provincial Championship rolled around, Hunter had settled on Timu at fullback and Paul Cooke and me on the wings. Though I still thought of myself as a fullback, I certainly didn't mind playing on the wing — in fact, I was delighted. I would have played anywhere for Otago, except perhaps in the front row.

My début for Otago – against South Canterbury in Timaru.

Timaru Herald

Otago teams have always been tight-knit, proud of their tradition and of "the Otago way" and anxious to add another layer of legacy for the next guys to come along. That team of 1993, or generally of the early 90s, did much to enhance the Otago image and to ensure tradition would not die with them. Every team, no matter who is in it or what the results, adds to the tradition and the lustre of a proud name, but that team seemed to do more than many. Though we had a few All Blacks in 1993 such as John Timu, Marc Ellis, Stephen Bachop, Stu Forster, Arran Pene and Jamie Joseph, it was the team as a whole and the attitude they brought to the game, both on and off the field, that made them more successful than you'd expect from talent alone. Among them were younger players such as myself, Josh Kronfeld, John Leslie, Taine Randell and Brendon Timmins who were able to carry on the traditions for the next generation. Otago does not have the playing depth in numbers of many provinces, but the spirit takes us along.

It was a good year, not just for me personally, but also for Otago. Though we lost a Ranfurly Shield challenge to Waikato, we beat them the following week in an NPC semifinal in Dunedin and though we lost to Auckland in the final, we'd also beaten them in the round-robin match at Carisbrook. Such is the enduring strength of Auckland rugby, and the aura they bring to their games, it's always a special day when they're beaten.

I know the Carisbrook crowd was rapt when we beat Auckland, the scarfies on the terrace going bananas and the walls of sound coming out from round the ground and seemingly hitting in the middle like tectonic plates heaving and buckling as they move the earth.

Much of the time, players are oblivious to what the crowd says or thinks, more so in rugby than in cricket. If you're concentrating totally on your game, as you should be, the crowd is just a background noise, sometimes picked up, sometimes not. When we beat Auckland, I don't know who was more delighted — the crowd or us. It certainly wasn't a comfortable victory; against Auckland it never is. We were well up at one stage, I think 18–3 or something, but you're never up against Auckland, you just have more points than they do for the moment. They're always capable of snapping back at you and if ever you start thinking you've got the game won, that's the time you start losing it.

Inevitably, they came back at us. Grant Fox kicked a couple of penalties and then John Kirwan scored a couple of tries. So much for our lead. We trailed 21-18 with 13 minutes to go. Was this to be another Dunkirk, another brave effort in defeat?

We were given a penalty 30 metres out from our line and ran it. Call it bold, call it stupid, it worked. Then another. Jamie Joseph had the ball and I screamed to him to tap and run. I was dreading the prospect of kicking for goal to tie the scores. I don't know (even still) if Jamie heard me, but he

The winning try against
Auckland. I celebrate
while Inga Tuigamala
doesn't look too
impressed.

tapped and went and threw a long pass to Paul Cooke. He made a few metres and was looking around for options just outside the 22 and I yelled for it. There were a few Auckland jerseys around but I just took off for the line; I was absolutely determined to score. Far easier than kicking to draw. I got around Inga Tuigamala and back inside Eroni Clarke and I was almost there when Shane Howarth came across at me. I tried to step him, caught him off-balance and my momentum carried me over the line as Waisake Sotutu joined in on the tackle. The try gave us the win but I was still nervous when I set up the conversion attempt. It was from wide out and I'd missed a couple of easier ones earlier. I started shaking as I lined the kick up. But it went over. Victory is always sweet. Even sweeter when it's against Auckland.

There was another kick that year that stayed in the memory, not because it gave us a win, but because it gave us a draw. It was against Wellington and a little explanation is needed here. Otago–Wellington matches are played for the Mike Gibson Memorial Trophy and, for some reason, it means a lot more to Otago players than it does to those from Wellington. Mike Gibson played for both Otago and Wellington in the 1980s and was, by all acounts, a very special sort of person. He was a distinctive player on the field with long hair often held in place by a headband and he looked the archetypal 1970s scarfie. He was very popular with his teammates and when he died of leukaemia, it was decided to have a trophy in his commemoration for matches between the two provinces.

Our coach, Gordon Hunter, as well as many of the players, had known Mike Gibson well and respected him enormously. I recall before the Wellington match at Athletic Park in 1993 Gordy got a little emotional — as he could do — as he was telling us what we were playing for, what it would have meant to Mike Gibson, and what it meant to him personally.

It's not fashionable these days to talk of winning at all costs, but that was almost what we were being exhorted to do. As it turned out, we were in dire danger of being beaten, playing into a fairly stiff southerly at Athletic Park in the second half and down 20-13. Paul Cooke, as only he could, plucked a try out of nowhere in the dying minutes and we were two points down with a minute to go. The conversion would give us the draw and it was up to me to take it. Into a southerly. Cooke had scored the try wide out and I was on or near the touchline as I lined it up. It was in front of the main stand and what sounded like hundreds of kids were going nuts behind me, willing me to miss it and give Wellington a win. I wasn't of a mind to give Wellington anything, least of all a win.

I took longer than usual to line it up, not to prolong the agony for fans of either side, but because kicking into the teeth of a southerly is not, as you can imagine, something goalkickers would want to do if they had a choice. I had no choice. Kick it over and draw, miss and lose.

As I began to move, the wind toppled the ball off its perch. Gleeful Wellington players rushed up and hoofed it downfield, as they were perfectly entitled to do. I was having none of this. I appealed to the referee, Jim Taylor of Counties. "Aw ref," I said in the time-honoured preface to conversations with such august officials, "I hadn't moved. I've got to have another shot."

Being an infinitely wise referee, well versed in the laws of the game, he agreed with me and allowed me a second attempt, without the distraction of Wellington players trying to charge it down.

It went over. Somehow.

A draw is never as good as a win and sometimes can be rudely frustrating, but this one was sweet. Because we held the Gibson trophy, the draw was sufficient to retain it. I swear there were tears in Gordy's eyes (eye?) when we got to the dressing room and I feared he was going to kiss me. He did embrace me.

There was no such joyous emotion from the other dressing room. Wellington's coach, David Kirk, muttered darkly that I had conned the referee because I had moved before the ball fell over.

Oh dear. Never mind. There's nothing better than beating people in their own stadium. Especially with such a prize at stake.

3. The Jersey

There have been nearly 1000 All Blacks and I can guarantee that every one of them retained in a special place in his memory the circumstances in which he first heard he had been chosen to play rugby for New Zealand. Some would have heard it on the radio, some in the public gaze of television, some in what Colin Meads once called the measured roll call of a team announcement under the grandstand at Athletic Park and there was one case, I heard, of the chosen players' names being written on a blackboard and it being propped up on the stage at a dance. You can imagine the flying wedge of players trying to get to the stage to see if their names were on the magic list.

It is a moment of satisfaction, fulfilment and joy, but also of some humility because every new All Black knows instantly the responsibility that has been bestowed upon him.

I was ecstatic when I was chosen for the New Zealand cricket team earlier in 1993, as anyone would be when chosen to represent their country in any sport, but with due respect to cricket and all the other sports, I think being named an All Black has an extra special edge to it. I suppose that is because the All Blacks mean so much to New Zealand as a whole and because historically they've been more successful than any other New Zealand team and more successful, I suspect, than most national teams anywhere from any sport. Maybe the Brazilian soccer team goes closest to the All Blacks' enduring feats of excellence, but I can't think of any other.

I became an All Black in Hamilton, though that's not strictly correct since no one becomes an All Black until he takes the field in world rugby's most recognised uniform. But I was in Hamilton when I heard I had been chosen for the All Blacks' tour of England and Scotland at the end of 1993.

Otago had had an unsuccessful Ranfurly Shield challenge against Waikato in the afternoon — we lost 28-11 — and I had been on the bench. We were a pretty subdued bunch afterward because we thought we had a team capable of winning the shield, but Waikato are a hard side to beat at Rugby Park in Hamilton, especially when the shield is at stake. You feel there that you're playing the crowd as well as the players on the field. We were in the team's court session back at the hotel when the manager, Gerard Simmons, was called out to the phone. He reappeared a few minutes later, stood up and asked the court for its indulgence, and said that seven of us, John Timu, Marc Ellis, Stephen Bachop, Stu Forster, Arran Pene, Jamie Joseph and myself, had been chosen for the All Black tour. For The Bear, Stu Forster, and me, it was the first time.

The subdued mood, which was gradually dissipating anyway as the court session unfolded, turned to one of jubilation. Backs were slapped, bodies were hugged, hands were shaken. I felt a strange sense of contentment and fulfilment tinged with the knowledge that I was now on the edge of the greatest challenge in my sporting life. Being chosen for the All Blacks was one thing. It was now up to me to justify that selection and to justify the faith the three selectors — Laurie Mains, Earle Kirton and Peter Thorburn — had in me. Selection is not an end in itself. It is the first step toward being a good All Black or, even better, a great All Black. There's a burning desire not to let The Jersey down. That's the challenge every player feels.

But amid the jubilation, there was also some sadness as there inevitably is in a selection process which sees some chosen and some not. The Hawke's Bay boys in the team, and there were a few at the time, felt for Paul Cooke, who had been playing well in 1993 and was thought to have been verging on making the All Blacks. I too felt for him because I was chosen in the position that he would have been. It could be said that I took his place. I felt too for John Kirwan, one of the great All Blacks and a player who had the respect of everyone, because I'd been picked ahead of him. He'd scored more tries in tests than any other New Zealander and he'd been an All Black fixture for nearly a decade, but he wasn't wanted. Not for the first time and not for the last, I wondered about the selectors' reasoning but didn't wonder for too long because that is a fruitless exercise. Selectors do what they do. It's not for us mere mortals to try to understand.

Each of us had to stand in the court session and make some comment about our selection. I was fairly new to the Otago scene still and didn't usually have much to say and just stood and said that naturally I was pleased, but that it was a shame Paul Cooke didn't make it.

I'd felt beforehand that I had a reasonable chance of selection but didn't know they were taking only

Selectors for some reason are always called the wise men. Here's the three of them from 1993, Peter Thorburn, Earle Kirton and Laurie Mains.

Photosport

three wings and never dreamt I would be preferred ahead of Kirwan. There was media talk about my chances and no matter how much you try to block that sort of talk out, some of it penetrates. I'd played well during the year for Otago and done some flashy things but mostly in my favour I think was that I hadn't done anything wrong, especially things selectors notice such as missing tackles you should make, knocking on all the time, getting caught out of position, that sort of stuff.

The selections had to be looked at in the context of Mains' long-term plans, and I was able to do that later with all the wisdom of hindsight. It was clear that Mains, who had taken over as coach the year before, was already thinking of the World Cup in South Africa and was wanting to blood new players he knew would be around, or could be around, for a few years. But he had to balance that with experience for the present because the All Black reputation is always at stake and there were two tests to be won, not to mention the midweek games in which, in Britain anyway, the sole aim seems to be stopping the All Blacks from scoring by whatever means possible.

As soon as I could after the court session, I spoke to Mum and Dad in Invercargill. They'd already heard the news and, naturally, they were delighted for me. Dad had always joked about carrying my bags for me on a tour of Britain but he'd been thinking of cricket rather than rugby. He was prepared to change, though! His advice was sage as always — just do your best and enjoy yourself.

Later that night, there was more hilarity as Ellis and Timu had their heads shaved, fulfilling a pact between the two that if the shield match was lost, they'd go bald. There was a certain wariness among other players who feared they might get dragged into shedding their locks too.

Hairless John Timu (left) and Marc Ellis.

We gained some measure of revenge for losing the shield challenge by beating Waikato well in the NPC semifinal at Carisbrook the following week — with me restored to the wing and goalkicking duties — though we lost the final to Auckland a week later.

And so the tour. Was it enjoyable? Being an All Black was but it's difficult to describe a tour of Britain as enjoyable. It was intense because it was a 13-match tour and we had only 30 players, which meant guys had to double up from Saturday matches to midweek matches. I know that used to be the norm on tours and on some there were only 26 players, but it's still difficult. It means that as a player it's not possible to switch off for a day or two, to relax and recharge the batteries. No sooner is one game out of the way than you're preparing for another that's only three or four days away. I know that, as players, we were thankful when John Hart was able to persuade the New Zealand union in 1996 of the logic of taking 36 players on tour. That meant players weren't having to play twice a week but there was still the opportunity for the so-called midweek players to force their way into the test team.

That was how I regarded myself at the start of the tour of England and Scotland. I was a new All Black and I considered it my job, my responsibility, to play as well as I could to put pressure on the established test players. Realistically, I knew that if I played reasonably well I would be considered for the test team because with Mains preferring Timu at fullback, the only other wings in contention were Va'aiga Tuigamala and Eric Rush.

I became something of a focus of attention on the tour because of my age and because I had played cricket for New Zealand, and the All Blacks' media man, Ric Salizzo, received more requests for interviews with me than for any other player. Phrases such as "Willie the Kid", "Roy of the Rovers", "The Wizard" and other adaptations of comic book heroes turning their dreams of sporting glory into reality all became a little tiresome, though I had to acknowledge that the press guys had a job to do and, as far as I was concerned, they were pretty kind. Downright flattering in some instances. The constant interviewing can be a distraction and at times an irritant and I soon learned to turn them down or to take several interviews all at once.

The attention wasn't just from the media. Before I'd left New Zealand, among the messages of congratulations I had received was a letter from Colin Cowdrey, the great England cricketer who is now a peer, who told me that he was also a rugby fan and that he looked forward to meeting me. To be noticed by such a renowned figure was nice, but I didn't think much more about it until I was introduced to him at a lunch at the British Sportsman's Club, one of those traditional English occasions that are always fitted into tours. We chatted a bit about rugby and cricket and he invited me to Lord's for a look around and while I would have loved to have gone there and soaked up a bit of the cricket atmosphere, there just wasn't time to fit it in.

The tour began with a bit of a hiss and a roar for me in the first game at Twickenham, against London Division. It was a bright and breezy sort of game in front of a full house — as full as Twickenham could be at the time because the new East stand had only just been opened and sections of it were still closed — and was played at a fairly hectic speed. The London team was as willing to attack as we were, which is not something I could say for the rest of the opposition on the tour. We wanted to play expansive rugby and were able to against London, but not able to in any of the other games, which must have made them fairly dreary for spectators. They were pretty dreary for the players at times too.

I was able to score a try in each half, being on the end of some smart work by the team and I could have had a third but for one of those funny moments that happen in matches from time to time. Toward the end of the game, when we'd established a lead and were pretty safe, Matthew Cooper and then Stu Forster attacked from almost on our own line. Forster passed to Sean Fitzpatrick at about halfway and as he charged toward the goal-line, all that was between him and a spectacular try was the London fullback, Huw Davies. I was outside Fitzpatrick and made sure he knew I was there. But instead of passing when he reached Davies, he ran straight into him and the ball was lost forward. Fitzpatrick laughed later that he'd thought he might do a Whineray — a reference to the occasion in 1964 when Wilson Whineray scored against the Barbarians after throwing an outrageous dummy. When

Five-point landing ... scoring on début for the All Blacks at Twickenham.

Daily Mail

the move died, Fitzpatrick said he wanted a hole to swallow him up and he yelled out to the touch judge, "Hey, you got a spade so I can dig a hole?"

Of course I wasn't complaining. He was the captain, after all. I was just the boy. Whatever Fitzpatrick decided was fine by me.

It had been an enjoyable game and had been a good start for me and I think, from that point on, Mains had me in mind for the tests. The rugby became less enjoyable, though, and the atmosphere of the tour wasn't helped by the unremitting grey skies you get in England. I know it's only the weather and the English can't do any more about their weather than we can about ours, but a combination of depressing overcast day after day allied to the negative way the other English sides played took much of the enjoyment out of the tour.

It was in the next game, at Redruth in Cornwall, that Philip de Glanville received a gash under an eye in a ruck and, for the British press at least, that became a continuing issue as the All Blacks were categorised as thugs and cheats and the English, of course, were the gallant, innocent victims. Mains and Fitzpatrick bore the brunt of the name calling and the accusations and for the rest of us, it was just a case of getting on with the tour. The de Glanville incident led to the absurdity though of what was grandly called a ruck summit, the English union insisting on a meeting with the New Zealand management over what was and was not legitimate in a ruck. The meeting was put off and put off and it all became a bit of a joke until finally it was held in London toward the end of the tour. It was held in a hotel function room called the Ashburn Room and the irony of the name didn't escape Mains. There is an Ashburn Hall in Dunedin that cares for the psychologically disturbed. Mains and the All Black manager, Neil Gray, had to agree to this absurd statement being made public:

". . . In the coaching and playing of the game, the intention of rucking is to get the ball by driving over it and raking it back. It is not the intention to deliberately trample on players and all players are coached to avoid contact with the head. That practice is abhorred by all of us."

This English inanity, for all its serious purpose because none of us likes seeing players get injured and none of us intends to inflict injury, became one of the lighter moments of the tour.

The internal pressures of the tour, that is, those imposed by the itinerary and the size of the touring party and the need to train and travel on the day after games, were very real and not like the peripheral external pressures. We could ignore the latter, and I hardly looked at a British paper for the whole tour, but we couldn't ignore the former. Mains was conscious that we needed a break — he was a very astute judge of the mood of a team and he had a good instinct for knowing when to apply the pressure or when to relax it. He decided to relax it in Liverpool, after the game against the North that we played at Anfield, the Liverpool soccer stadium. Playing there in itself was a pleasant break from the routine of the tour because it was a novelty playing at a ground we'd heard so much about and also because the Liverpool club's facilities were much better than what's normally found at English rugby grounds, particularly those where the midweek matches are usually staged.

We had the usual court session after the game back at our hotel and it went on . . . and on . . . I didn't drink at that stage of my career mainly because I didn't like the taste of beer. It might have been just as well because I don't know how long I would have lasted. It was one of the heavier All Black sessions in which I've been involved. I think it went on for about three hours and then, for those hardy souls for whom enough was never enough, it continued in the adjacent bar of the hotel. Mains chose that night because it was the longest gap we had between games — the following match at Gateshead wasn't until the Sunday — and because he said we'd worked hard in the first fortnight of the tour, which we had.

Some of the New Zealand journalists on the tour were in the next-door bar during the court session and they told us later of how, as the singing and yelling from behind the closed doors got louder, hotel staff scurried around moving reproduction antique furniture from the bar and took down light fittings. They must have heard the stories about teams that had pulled hotels apart like the 1968 Lions in South Africa who became known as The Wreckers, and were worried what we'd do to their fine establishment. But the hotel was in no danger. All Blacks have seldom, if ever, been like that and if there have been odd instances of furniture being damaged, it's been individuals and not the collective will of the team. Besides, there were several non-drinkers such as myself, Va'aiga Tuigamala and Eroni Clarke to keep an eye out in case something might have gone wrong and later, in the bar, a couple of players were designated as policemen who had to ensure that order and decorum were maintained.

All that was wrecked in the bar, as it turned out, was the tune of that old country song, *Stand By Your Man*. It happened that the woman who had a hit with the song, Tammy Wynette, was also staying in the hotel and she arrived back from a concert at nearby Southport just as the court session was finishing. Being a woman wise in the ways of the world, she kept on walking across the foyer, past the bar, into the lift and up to her room, never to be seen by All Blacks again. Some of her road crew, however, went to the bar and a few players and journalists decided to entertain them with Wynette's best-known song. Some had trouble with the words, more had trouble with the tune, and none of the road crew, it has to be said, rushed in with Nashville contracts.

All Black teams had had similar drinking sessions before — one most famously when Alex Wyllie as coach took the 1988 team into a league club

bar in Sydney and many hours later poured them on to their bus — and they do no harm provided a measure of control is maintained. With Wyllie around, there would always have been control.

Rugby and beer have always been in a close association, partly because there is such a heavy brewery sponsorship of rugby but also partly because one of the things that sets rugby apart from other games is that it is still, even at the highest level, an opportunity to socialise with your teammates and your opponents. I can't speak from experience of course, but I understand that the drinking now is much more moderate than it used to be; it certainly is more moderate now than when I first came on the scene. Some teams then would think it a dry night if they'd demolished only two kegs after a game. And that was before setting out from the ground for the bars. Immediately after a game, players would reach for a beer — and some for a smoke — as soon as they got back to the dressing room and before they even took their sodden jerseys or boots off. That doesn't happen now. Fluid replacement means water or electrolytes or tea; not cans or bottles of beer.

Rugby is such an intense game, both physically and mentally, that there is a real need to wind down afterwards and I see nothing wrong with that, providing players are responsible and don't go over the top. Lurking in the back of players' minds should always be the next game and the amount of recovery time required.

There is also an element of tradition associated with drinking after a game. I had to drink three cans after my first game for Otago and though I didn't then like it, I did it. Now that I'm one of the back seat boys, I'm one of those who insist the new guys have to drink their jug or three cans or whatever it may be. Guys who are only on water, by preference or because the doctor has advised them not to drink, have to drink the same quantities of water as they would have beer. As one who has had to do that, drinking beer is a hell of a lot easier, I can tell you.

As with all things associated with top sport, drinking is a question of balance. Players know that as finely trained athletes, drinking copious amounts of beer is not doing them any good but they also know, or should, when to stop and how much recovery time to allow themselves. Individuals have to take responsibility for what they do. There have been some drinking-related incidents involving high-profile players and none of us condones such behaviour; what the rest of us have to do is to protect each other and ensure that nothing gets out of hand. I've followed guys around for two and a half years to make sure they didn't get themselves into trouble. Although I drink now, I've never been so drunk that I didn't know what I was doing. I'm lucky enough to know when to walk away and go home and if there are some who don't know that, the rest of us have to look after them. In Otago, we have a saying, "Always look after your mates," and that applies.

Anfield, Liverpool's famous soccer ground, saw kicking of a different style in 1993. This was my first kicking assignment for the All Blacks. Referee Jim Fleming and I follow the flight.

I have to say that there have been some incidents involving players in which the players, though drinking, have been more the victim than the villain. There are, unfortunately, people who seem to take pleasure out of taunting or baiting well-known rugby players as if they're in some sort of macho contest. "Ah, you're not as tough (or big, or smart) as you think you are." That sort of thing. The prudent player should always walk away, turn the other cheek, in such circumstances. Not all do and that's when the trouble starts.

From what I've been told, the number of players getting involved in late-night incidents hasn't increased in recent years. What has increased is the media coverage of them. It only needs a player to step out of line, or be forced out of line, for a relatively minor breach these days and it's all over the papers and on television. In earlier years, such incidents weren't reported. Perhaps that was because reporters were more tolerant and understanding, perhaps it was because society was more tolerant, or perhaps it was because the authorities, either police or team managements or rugby union administration, kept it all quiet. There are a great many more news media outlets now than there were — as players being asked for interviews know only too well — and in a competitive world, a newspaper or a television station feels it has to be more aggressive to retain its position in the marketplace.

Even in my time, I knew of an incident involving two All Blacks who had to appear in court the day before leaving for a tour overseas. The police and court staff combined to keep it all quiet and their misdemeanour, as minor as it was, has forever remained away from the public knowledge.

There was no need for anything like that in Liverpool, though, just a few sore heads and a very quiet bus the next day as we went across the Pennines to Gateshead.

Before we'd left Liverpool, though, we learnt a bit about an All Black from the past at breakfast. Our manager, Neil Gray, had invited to breakfast two daughters and a grandson of one of the 1905 All Blacks, George Smith, and Gray had told us that it would be appreciated if there could be a good turnout of players to meet these people. Sean Fitzpatrick was playing the charming host as we sat there and heard about this guy who not only played for the All Blacks, but who also was a New Zealand and British sprint champion, was in the first New Zealand league team and had even ridden the winner of a New Zealand Cup. I was sitting a table away and in the background a bit when Frank Bunce yelled across the tables, "Hey Goldie, here's a guy who could do more than even you." Everyone laughed, but it was a bit embarrassing. It's when a current All Black, whose knowledge of rugby history is not usually very extensive, hears of such players from the past that the enduring value of the All Blacks really hits home. You feel proud to be a part of such a lineage.

By the time of the game at Gateshead against England A, it was apparent that Mains had pretty much decided on his lineup for the test against Scotland that was still a fortnight away. Though there's usually media and public speculation about who could play and who is or is not in contention, the players usually either know or get a pretty good feel for what's going on.

Among the changes Mains had signalled was the selection of Marc Ellis at first five-eighth ahead of a specialist in that position, Stephen Bachop. It was a decision that was criticised, even ridiculed, back in New Zealand but Mains and Earle Kirton knew what they were doing. Ellis was a very talented footballer and suffered because of that talent. He could play just about anywhere in the backs and he became tagged as a utility player, someone to fill in when others were either injured or out of form. Had Ellis been able to develop fully in a position he could call his own, he may have turned out to be a great All Black and may not have been tempted to league at the end of 1995. First five-eighth may have been that position. Kirton remembered him playing there when he was at school in Wellington and felt that was his rightful position and, not only that, but that he could become the permanent All Black first-five. We'll never know because after playing in the tests against England and Scotland, he was injured the following year and by the time he was ready for consideration again, Andrew Mehrtens had burst onto the scene and Simon Culhane was right behind him. Ellis therefore reverted to his spare part role and drifted away to league.

I felt that he played well at first-five in the Scottish test, particularly because it was a game suited to his style. The more structured test a week later against England tested him more, but that game would have tested any first-five.

Scotland was a stark contrast to England. We travelled by bus from Gateshead to Peebles in the Scottish Borders region and by coincidence, as we crossed the border into Scotland, the sun broke out. The players cheered. It was a good omen for the fortnight we spent there. We felt much more at home in Scotland than we had in England; people seemed friendlier and there was less media antagonism toward the All Blacks. Even Mains, who could have a face like thunder at times, seemed to unwind and got around with a smile on his face. That may have had something to do with him being able to indulge in one of his favourite pastimes, fishing. Though the Scottish leg of the tour was just as organised and just as intensive as it had been in England, we felt more relaxed and we were able to get away from rugby for short times. A major reason for that was that Edinburgh is a relatively compact city and to visit Edinburgh Castle, for example, was just a short stroll up the Royal Mile from our hotel. If we'd wanted to do any touristy things in London, it would have meant hours sitting in the bus. So I had the obligatory photos taken of myself leaning on an ancient cannon or looking out over Edinburgh from the castle's battlements, just like a regular tourist on his OE.

The Scottish test was a dream début. Everything just fell into place for me. I was nervous before the game but they were more nerves because of the size of the occasion rather than nerves of apprehension. I'd been playing reasonably well and, anyway, there should always be an element of tension before a test, no matter who the opponent is. Players think about the game as a whole and their role in it, anxious not to let their team and their teammates down; they think about the total elimination of mistakes. Before a first test, there's also a sense of not knowing. Though I'd played in some big rugby matches, none had been a test and I'd heard from other players how tests are another step up and that they're so much faster and harder. Some players find it difficult after tests to recall exactly what happened when. It all goes by in a blur and it's only when you watch a tape of it later that you can get a real sense of what happened.

For me, with No 14 on my back in a test for the first time, part of my preparation and motivation was to think of other All Blacks who had worn the No 14 and how I couldn't disgrace their legacy. Most of all I thought of John Kirwan, whose No 14 I was wearing on this tour.

I somehow get the ball back to Zinzan Brooke against Scotland. Marc Ellis, Frank Bunce, Andy Nicol and Rob Wainwright all wanted part of the action.

Colorsport/Olympix

All test grounds are different although they are just patches of grass on which rugby is played. I don't get carried away with the atmosphere and traditions of grounds and, in 1993, the grounds to me were just like any other, especially because Twickenham and Murrayfield were both going through rebuilding at the time. Murrayfield in particular didn't feel like a stadium renowned for its atmosphere, not even when the crowd sang *Flower of Scotland* accompanied by massed pipers. It was more like a construction site. We got changed in a temporary dressing room away from the stands and we had to reach it by walking over newly laid planks. The "main" stand was more a tent erected on scaffolding just for the one match and the royal guests of honour, Princess Anne and Prince Edward, sat on the temporary board seats just like everyone else.

We were introduced to Princess Anne before the game and when she shook my hand — or did I shake hers? I'm not sure of the royal protocol — she made some remark to me about how cold it was. "You're not wrong," I replied.

People who'd told me it would pass in a blur and a flash were right, but it was also a fast game anyway, helped along by both the All Blacks and the Scots determined on a positive, expansive style of play. It was one of those games in which things went for me — even the refereeing decisions! The pass I received from Frank Bunce for my first try was later said to have been forward but the referee, Freek Burger from South Africa, didn't rule it and I

I acknowledge the try I didn't want against Scotland and Stu Forster, the man responsible for it, seems to be scratching his head in wonderment.

wasn't hanging around to debate it. My second came from a kick through by John Timu and it was just a straight race between Scott Hastings and me. And the third was thanks to Stu Forster, though I'd told him I didn't want it. He'd called a blindside move from a scrum not far out from the Scottish line and I asked Stu to change the call because I was feeling a bit knackered and wondered if I'd make it. He said he was calling it anyway, the ball came to me, and it's amazing how the tiredness slips away when you've got the ball in your arms.

That was the try I also had to try to convert because Matthew Cooper had left the field with the thigh injury that would eventually keep him out of the England test. The try had got us up to 49 points and I remember thinking as I placed the ball that it was up to me to crack the 50. I had visions of headings saying "Wilson fails!" if I'd missed it but I hit it pretty well and it sailed over.

So that was my first test. Three tries and a conversion and as personally satisfying as they were, it's the team effort that brings the real satisfaction and I felt the All Blacks that day were in commanding form, especially in the forwards. But the Scots deserved more credit for their display than the final score of 51-15 indicated. If it's entertaining rugby that's in demand, both teams have to want to entertain. The Scots did their bit.

Not so in England. The games there were dour because of the negative, spoiling way the English teams played and in some of them I hardly touched the ball. In the test against England, I sometimes wish I hadn't. It wasn't that I played badly, or even that the All Blacks played badly, it was just that England played a no-risk game better than we did. It was a loss that hurt the All Blacks, though, and England paid for it two years later in the World Cup semifinal in Cape Town. It hurt me too because as the goalkicker I had an added responsibility and no matter which way it's looked at, I didn't do that part of my job. We may have won if I'd had a better success rate with my kicking but we'll never know that. The fact is we lost and I felt it more than most. I was bitterly disappointed afterward and sat in the dressing room and cried. Some of the players made an attempt to cheer me up, to tell me that it's teams that lose tests, not individuals, but Mike Brewer told them to leave me alone, that I had to learn to lose. It was a valuable, if painful, lesson. I've learned to take losses a lot more philosophically since, but I still hate losing.

Brewer's presence in the dressing room was a cause for some controversy at home, but none at all within the team. He had been unavailable for the tour but had been in England representing the apparel sponsors, Canterbury International. He joined up with us when we were down in Cornwall and was virtually a part of the tour from then on, though he was never an official member of the party. Our loose forward complement was depleted in the match in Gloucester before the England test when Paul Henderson was

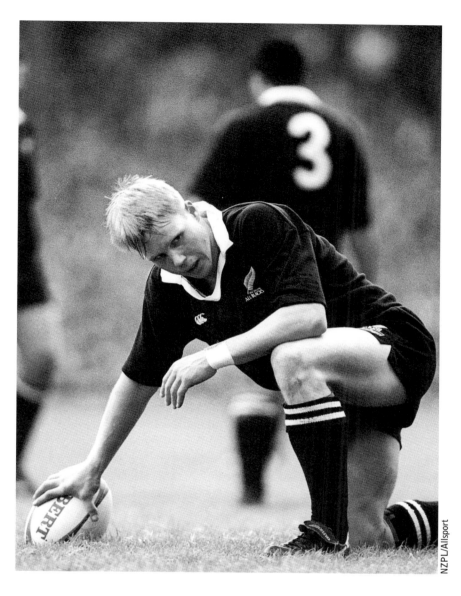

NZPL/Allsport

The England test held no happy memories.

injured. This would have meant that Liam Barry would have gone into the test reserves but, instead, Mains called Brewer in after first checking with Neil Gray and the chairman of the New Zealand union, Eddie Tonks, if this was acceptable. Mains' rationale was that Brewer was vastly experienced and that Barry, on his first tour as an All Black, was not. So Brewer sat as a reserve during the England test and a week later went on as a reserve against the Barbarians in Cardiff. I can understand how Barry was upset, feeling that an outsider denied him a chance, but I could also understand Mains' view. Brewer, it was widely known, would have been made captain in 1992 had he not been injured in the final trial and Mains had to turn to Fitzpatrick

Liam Barry attacks against the Scottish Development team in Edinburgh.

instead. For much of the time that Brewer was an All Black, even when Alex Wyllie was still the coach, he was an authoritative figure within the team and at times was almost the surrogate captain. Very little happened within All Black teams in those days without Brewer being consulted first.

I was just an observer to all of this in 1993. As the baby of the team, I just kept quiet and spoke when I was spoken to. Not for me the intrigues of the back seat boys!

It was a good two years later, though, when Liam Barry finally got his test chance, against France in Paris, and took it well. Justice was seen to be done.

The loss to England ensured that the tour ended on an unhappy note, even though we had two matches after that, finishing with the win against the Barbarians. Such are the standards required of — and by — the All Blacks, that if tests are lost, no matter what else is achieved, it's the losses that set the tone and which will be remembered.

Just to ensure that we left England with unhappy memories the England captain, Will Carling, compounded the situation when he wrote a newspaper column on our final day, saying rugby's image was wrecked by the All Blacks.

"If they had beaten England," he wrote, "they would have been remembered as an all-conquering team. Now they will be remembered mostly as a dirty side. That is sad for them, but I think they deserve it."

Talk about sour grapes from a winning captain. He was incensed by the de Glanville incident, which was an accident, and by Jamie Joseph standing on England halfback Kyren Bracken in the Twickenham test, which was less accidental and for which Joseph paid. But to call the All Blacks a dirty side was going way too far. If rugby's image was ruined, it was ruined by the negative, spoiling way in which the English teams — including Carling's — approached their games. The English are not my favourite rugby players, on the field or off it. If I never have to play in England again, I'll be happy.

The year of 1993 had been a special year for me and I haven't had another one like it. It was just a pity that it had to end on such a sour, bitter note.

4. Managing two jobs

Not being a particularly keen student of sporting history, I've had to rely on others to learn that I am New Zealand's seventh "double All Black". I put that in quotation marks because it is a misnomer. Strictly speaking, a double All Black would be someone who has been picked twice for the All Blacks, and there are hundreds of them.

But I suppose most people understand what is meant. A double All Black is someone who has played rugby and cricket for New Zealand, the two sports that are seen as the national winter and summer games. I think the description is demeaning of a great many people who have represented their country at two sports — or more — yet never get the same recognition. If an All Black has also played softball for New Zealand, such as Andy Leslie, or wrestled for New Zealand, such as Gary Knight, it just becomes a sporting footnote. If a New Zealand cricketer plays another sport, say Mark Burgess playing soccer for New Zealand, the same thing occurs.

Photosport

**Which will it be?
Rugby or cricket?**

63

They are but three examples of many.

The days of such versatility in sport, whatever the combination of sports, are all but over except for dual representation in allied sports such as cycling or athletics and triathlon, or perhaps a cricketer or an All Black in a later career also competing for New Zealand at something such as bowls or shooting, something that doesn't depend entirely on a relatively youthful body.

It seems fairly certain that I will be the last double All Black. I don't say that out of arrogance or out of some selfish desire to retain the exclusivity of such an élite club, but because it's just plain pragmatic common sense. Even history backs me up. Before I played both sports in 1993, the most recent double All Black was Brian McKechnie, whose All Black career covered the years 1977-81 and whose cricket career was spread between 1975 and 1981.

The last before him was Bill Carson before the Second World War, whose All Black career was confined to 1938 and whose cricket spanned the three years, 1937-39.

Of the other four double All Blacks, I'm told, one was in the 30s (Eric Tindill), two traversed the 20s and 30s (Charlie Oliver and Curly Page) and one was in the 20s (George Dickinson).

Of the seven of us, only one, Tindill, played tests in both sports. He was even more remarkable because when he finished playing, he went on to man in the middle status and became both a rugby test referee and a cricket test umpire. I can assure everyone, with no possible shadow of doubt or changed circumstances, that I will not be trying to emulate him. Whatever I do in sport later in my life, I will not be donning a white coat or blowing a whistle and drawing the shape of a television set in the air.

The five earlier double All Blacks played in eras that are barely recognisable by today's standards. Seasons for both were relatively short and, more significantly, they were clearly defined. Cricket was for the summer months and rugby for the winter. There was very little overlap, except when there was a tour to the northern hemisphere (which is when Tindill played his rugby test, in the 1935 match against England which was lost at Twickenham. There are a few modern All Blacks, myself included, who know exactly how that feels).

Those five, I imagine, would have finished playing cricket in March and then started playing club rugby, working their way up to playing representative matches in August and September, then had a month or six weeks off before gradually working their way into the cricket season. The demands then outside of the actual playing would have been minimal if not non-existent and, of course, they had regular jobs outside of their sports.

My admiration and respect for their achievements is not diminished and it's a fruitless exercise comparing different eras when society was different

Adding another sport to the repertoire – neither Tony Brown nor I seem too serious about this cross-training.

Photosport

and the games themselves were not as they are now, just as the games when they played them would not have been the same as they were 20 or 30 years earlier.

When we were in Britain in 1993, as I said earlier, we were told about one of the Original All Blacks, George Smith, who also was a champion sprinter and hurdler, winning New Zealand and British titles; he played in the first New Zealand league team (in fact, helped organise it) and, earlier in his career, he had also ridden the winner of a New Zealand Cup. He's not known as a double All Black because he didn't play cricket for New Zealand (though he may have played cricket for all I know) but he certainly did plenty else. Can you imagine a cup-winning jockey today becoming an All Black a couple of years later? No? Neither can I. An All Black owning a cup-winning horse, now that's different and much more likely. I hope it's me.

Different eras, different circumstances.

In this era and in these circumstances, it's hard to see anyone being able to play cricket and rugby for New Zealand again. It's not just a question of time, though that certainly comes into it. It's also a question of fitness and body shape. Training today is so specialised, much more than it ever has been. And training methods and theories will continue to develop, making it even less likely that athletes could pursue more than one sport other than for relaxation purposes, such as golf. My body is not a cricket body any more and if I were to have aspirations to resume cricket at a decent level, I would have to undergo a completely different training regimen and it may take me two or three years to get into the sort of physical shape that top cricket

Back in the middle, temporarily anyway. Batting in Dunedin's Octagon during a promotion with the New Zealand cricketers.

demands. By then, I could be too old! That's quite apart from the technical skills that would be required, and I would have to work hard on those as well. I may be too old now.

The rules would also have to change to allow someone to compete at the top level in both sports. Most top sports people are contracted to someone, rugby players to the New Zealand union and cricketers to New Zealand Cricket. The contracts specify that players must be available for national selection. It's hardly likely anyone good enough could be excused playing Super 12 or NPC or something to go off on a cricket tour, or for a cricketer to avoid the dubious delights of touring the sub-continent so he could stay home and play rugby. Sport is not structured like that any more, though my rugby contract always included a provision for me to be able to play cricket.

But even if a superman came along and could still do both, where would he find the time? How could a rugby player squeeze cricket practice (both team and individual) into the 11-month-a-year life of an All Black? With Otago and the Highlanders, we have a fairly intense cricket competition that we play in hotel carparks or whatever space we can find when we have the time, but that standard doesn't seem likely to attract the attentions of the national cricket selectors.

There is too the question of risk. I don't know what individual contracts other than mine say, but it's reasonable to assume that contracts for other rugby players specify what they can and can't do. I know the Rugby Union would frown if I had a yearning (which I don't) to jump out of perfectly good aeroplanes with a parachute strapped to my back. I don't imagine any of our national cricketers would be allowed to go and play rugby and risk injury which not only would affect their livelihood, but also affect the financial wellbeing of New Zealand Cricket.

During the buildup phase to the Super 12 in 2000, I went to Carisbrook on a Saturday to catch up with a few old friends playing in an Otago–Auckland Shell Trophy match. Auckland through one reason or another were down on numbers and their captain, Blair Pocock, asked me if I'd field. I jumped at the chance. I made sure I stationed myself on the fine leg–third man boundary and I also took great care to ensure that anything requiring a dive into the fence or a prodigious leap was left well alone (I was fielding for Auckland against Otago, after all). It was all a bit of harmless fun. The Auckland guys were glad of what help I was able to give them and the Otago guys thought me wearing an Auckland cap was a huge joke.

A couple of days later, the Highlanders manager, Des Smith, received a phone call from a radio station asking if the Highlanders were mounting an inquiry into me playing cricket. An inquiry into what? There was nothing to inquire into. Yes, I played cricket, if roaming the boundary could be called playing cricket.

Smith replied well. He said that the Highlanders were encouraged to pursue interests outside of rugby and that he had faith in my maturity and responsibility not to put myself or my rugby at risk. I would have been more at risk crossing the road.

The couple of hours or so I spent on the field, though, were a good reminder to me that I didn't have a cricket body any more.

People have raised with me a few times the fact that the only two double All Blacks of modern times, Brian McKechnie and me, have been from Southland and why did I think that was so? I've no idea. It's probably more coincidence than anything else, though I do know from my own experience that sport during my school days in Invercargill was greatly encouraged and was something very enjoyable, and I imagine that for McKechnie, growing up in a similar environment to me but a few years earlier, it would have been much the same. I don't think that would be a lot different from most other places in New Zealand though. I think it probably helped that in cricket in Invercargill there are two aspirant levels, the Hawke Cup or whatever name it goes by now at district level, and the Otago team at the Shell Trophy level.

As I've said, I was never a great sports follower, more a doer, and it was only in later years that I came to know some of the detail of McKechnie's career and it was only later that I got to know him as well. It almost defies belief what he got himself involved in. I had to agree with the introduction to his book, *McKechnie — Double All Black*, which said that if any novelist had dreamed up McKechnie's achievements, the plot would have been dismissed as improbable. He was a replacement on both the 1978 All Blacks' tour of Britain — a replacement in the match as well — and on the 1980-81 cricket tour of Australia when he was a central figure in two celebrated incidents in New Zealand sport. The first was him kicking the penalty that gave the All Blacks the win against Wales after the infamous (and inconsequential) lineout dive and the second was that he was the recipient of Trevor Chappell's underarm delivery. I've been involved in a bit of controversy in my time, but my little efforts pale in the shadows of his.

Even in McKechnie's time, when rugby was still amateur and when cricketers were paid a pittance compared with today, playing both sports for New Zealand was an incredible achievement. And all the while, he had a "normal" job as an accountant in Invercargill. His employers were clearly more supportive and understanding of the extreme demands on his time than many employers would be today. But perhaps that was the Southland way, where people are parochially proud of their sporting heroes and get in behind them in every way they can. The success of the Southern Sting in the Coca-Cola Cup netball is a modern example of how Southlanders, both businesses and individuals, support their sports people. It will be good when Homestead Stadium is redeveloped so Southland can truly embrace the Highlanders.

I'm often asked if I dreamt of playing cricket and/or rugby for New Zealand and the answer is no, I didn't. In the backyard games Richard and I used to play, sometimes we were New Zealand or Australia and sometimes we'd hit the winning runs or score the winning try, but that was no different to what generations of New Zealand boys and girls have done and, I hope, will continue to do. When I reached the stage of knowing that I had more than the average ability at some sports, I never consciously thought, "One day I'll play for New Zealand." The ambition, from as early as I can remember, was to play for the next level up from what I was playing at the time. I don't think in either sport did I ever look beyond the next level. Dad was always good at telling me to set goals that I could achieve because unachievable goals weren't worth striving for. So if I was in the Hawke Cup team, for example, my ambition was to make the Shell Trophy team. When I was in the Southland rugby team and, the following year, in the Otago team, the goal was to get into the Colts or the Divisional team or to get an All Black trial. It was only when I was at the trial level that I thought about being an All Black. But, and I think this is important, I didn't think to myself: "I'd love to be chosen for the All Blacks." What I thought instead was: "I'd love to be playing well enough to get selected for the All Blacks." There is a difference.

I think it was necessary to get the proper grounding at one level before

attempting to move on to the next and there was also a lot of proving to be done — proving to myself most of all that what I could do at one level, I could also do at the next level up.

Another thing working against the possibility of there being another double All Black is one big factor in the huge changes rugby has undergone in the last four or five years, and that's the length of tours. Rugby is now geared almost exclusively toward tests and it was rare for me, or any other modern All Black, to play anything for New Zealand other than a test. The statistics alone tell the story. By the end of 1999, I had played 54 tests but only 11 other games for New Zealand. Josh Kronfeld and Andrew Mehrtens are even more extreme examples. Kronfeld by the end of 1999 had played 47 tests but only two other games for New Zealand; Mehrtens had played 39 tests and also only another two. Contrast that with Bryan Williams who played 113 matches for New Zealand, but only 38 of them were tests or, to give the ultimate example, Colin Meads who played an

A photo that needs no caption. Trevor Chappell bowls his infamous delivery to Brian McKechnie. It may be just as well we can't see the umpire's face.

extraordinary 133 games for New Zealand, but of these, only 55 were tests.

The point is that on the tours of earlier years, 30 matches in some extreme cases and, as an example, 18 on the 1978 Grand Slam tour, All Blacks could play 10 or 12 or even more matches without playing a test. On the tours we go on now, either there aren't any non-test matches or when there are, we have sufficient players so we don't have to double up. It would have been possible (and was) in earlier years, when there were longer tours and more strictly defined seasons, for a cricketer to be an All Black. It's not now.

There is too almost an indecent haste for teenagers to be rushed into top rugby. It's common now for schoolboys to be targeted by unions and they go into "the system", playing age grade rugby then being contracted by a provincial union and by the national union for either sevens or Super 12. They'd be far better going at their own pace and playing club rugby and gaining experience before moving so quickly to the top level. There are some younger All Blacks, experienced already at Super 12 level, who have probably had more first-class games than they have had club games. Their exposure so soon in their lives to top rugby also hasn't left them time to play any other sport to a higher level. Or, for that matter, given them much opportunity to experience other sides of life.

It's increasingly evident that if someone hasn't been chosen for the All Blacks by their mid-20s at the latest, they're never going to make it. This works against late-maturing players and the most common example is front row players, who can be at their best in their late 20s or even early 30s. There was a time when national selectors would look to players of that age group, but they don't seem to any more. Just look at the Highlanders and All Black front row of Anton Oliver, Carl Hoeft and Kees Meeuws. Each of them is in his mid-20s and they have been playing together now for four years. If the theory of older props being better is true, other teams had better watch out because we've yet to see the best of my Otago teammates. When older players have seen the writing on the wall and know that selection for the All Blacks has passed them by, they either look overseas or they give the game away, thus depriving club rugby of a vast store of experience. I know that it's an increasing concern in both rugby and cricket that, at club level, there isn't the same depth of older, experienced talent that there used to be. It's not just a problem in New Zealand. I know the English union, which at élite level has made a bit of a mess of running professional rugby, has deep concerns about dwindling adult numbers in club rugby and early in 2000 launched a comprehensive inquiry into the reasons.

Sport does not have the sole answer of course. No matter how well or effectively a sport is run, there are more options for young people than there ever were, either through other sports or other ways in which they may want to spend their leisure time.

5. Chasing dreams

If 1993 was the year of sport in the dress circle, 1994 was the year of the cheap seats. There was no doubt that 1993 had been my best year because it included the firsts of playing cricket and rugby for New Zealand so of course they couldn't be repeated. It was, as they say, a hard act to follow and I knew that whatever else I would do in sport, I couldn't have another year like 1993.

But I hadn't planned on having a 1994 in which not an awful lot went right, some of it through my own doing and some of it not. They reckon that sport is a good builder of character as you learn the lessons of success one day and failure the next, adulation one day and criticism the next. If that's the case, my character took on several more levels during 1994.

It started in unusual and somewhat mysterious circumstances in which I was just a distant party, learning what had happened after the event and then just laughing it off anyway.

It concerned the annual sports awards in which I had apparently been nominated for Sportsman of the Year and for the Fair Play award for my efforts in 1993. I say "apparently" because I had no knowledge of any of this. The Halberg Trust, founded by that great athlete, Sir Murray Halberg, to recognise excellence in sport at the same time as raising funds for crippled children, has done a great job over the years. The way the system works is that the trust's voting academy nominates people and teams for the various categories, then votes on them, and the top four in each category get invited to the awards dinner. The academy ranks each group of four and the winners, plus the overall winner of the Halberg Award, are announced on the night. The first I heard of any of this was when I was contacted by the trust and told I was a finalist in the two awards, Sportsman of the Year and Fair Play. The dinner was at the Viaduct Basin in Auckland with the "top table" on what looked like a floating barge, with all the rest of the dinner guests surrounding them in a U-shape on the wharves. It would have been a great idea if it had been a balmy evening, but it poured the whole night. Most of the dinner guests were lashed with wind and rain and the weather also played havoc with the sound and video systems, making it almost impossible for most guests to see or hear what was going on. The night was not a roaring success.

I didn't go there with any great expectations. Winning awards, especially those organised by the Halberg Trust, is all very well and if I'd won I would have felt humble and honoured, but it's a subjective thing decided by people far removed from me. The judges have to choose between different people from different sports and how on earth do you compare, for example, me with Russell Coutts or Danyon Loader or Philip Tataurangi, who were the other finalists. Tataurangi was named the winner and I was entirely happy with that.

The Fair Play award was a different story, as I discovered that night. I had been selected along with golfer Bob Charles, yachtsman Brad Butterworth and cricketer John Wright. The basis of fair play awards is the dictum of playing hard but fair and I have no problem with that because that is the way I try to play, as do most sports people that I know. The award sometimes, though, came across as a consolation award, something to give to someone who was deserving but who missed out on the top award. I didn't mind that either. It was harmless enough.

The award that night went to Butterworth who had evidently been competing in a yacht race and sacrificed his own chances of winning to help a yacht that was in distress. He was a good choice. That's the sort of thing that fair play awards should reward. I'm not a great fan of fair play awards because I come from the school that believes that in sport the nice guys finish last. Fair play awards are a laudable scheme, but winning is what competition is all about.

(Butterworth himself a few years later had a harsh lesson in how public perceptions change when he was the focus of disfavour for leaving Team New Zealand.)

But I learned at the dinner that, in the voting process, I had actually been decided the winner but that the result of the vote had been changed some time between the voting taking place and the dinner, supposedly because of some unpublicised misdemeanour of mine. I learnt, amid the wind and the rain at the dinner, that the result had been altered because of "errant" behaviour by me in a Shell Trophy cricket match that summer. Missing out on the award didn't bother me because Butterworth was a worthy winner, but the circumstances of how things changed were annoying. It seemed to me that some people had heard half a story here and half a story there and, without checking with me, acted as if what they had been told were the indisputable facts.

The facts were fairly simple. I don't deny that I am a hard competitor. What's the point playing in any sport if you don't give of everything you've got? Neither do I deny that I'm not averse to giving a bit of lip to an opponent in the heat of the moment.

I'd been playing for Otago in the trophy match against Canterbury at Dudley Park in Rangiora and Nathan Astle was batting. The Otago guys were getting more than a bit frustrated because he was playing and missing a hell of a lot yet was still able to slowly build up runs to reach his maiden half-century. When he was eventually out, I and several of my teammates sent him on his way, to use the favoured cricket term for when a dismissed batsman is fondly farewelled by the guys in the field. I shouted something at his departing back — I can't remember what — and spat in his general direction. Spitting, you may have noticed, is now a common occurrence in sport as athletes rid themselves of excessive amounts of saliva built up through exercise.

Someone in the Canterbury team complained that I had spat at Astle, the umpires got involved and eventually the Otago coach, Lance Cairns, told me I'd better apologise to him. I did say sorry to Astle, but it was the most insincere apology anyone could have delivered and I think Astle was as bemused by it all as I was. It was a bit like a rugby referee telling a couple of hulking props to shake hands after they'd had a go at each other in a scrum. Anyone who has ever seen that happen knows that the hands are not shaken with a great deal of heartfelt conviction. If I'd wanted to spit at him, and if I'd been any good at spitting, I would have hit him with it and maybe then an apology would have had some meaning. But I'm not much good at spitting and I didn't spit at him so it was all a minor little drama over nothing.

I'm no angel on the field. I shout and I swear when things don't go my way and that's a part of my competitive nature. But I don't attack individuals. I never have and never will. That's not what sport is about for me. The other thing about such incidents is that they happen out in the middle when guys are fired up and it's out in the middle they should remain. It's what happens in the heat of the battle and if people expect such incidents to be eradicated from games altogether, I fear for the future of sport.

So that was my only brush with the fair play award and, needless to say, I haven't been a contender for it since. It is not something that keeps me awake at nights.

My rugby year in 1994 began soon after, with a tour of Argentina that does not sit highly among my rugby memories. The team was grandly known as a New Zealand Development team and I have no idea what the Rugby Union was thinking when it put the team together. I suspect Argentina had wanted a full New Zealand team, which had last toured there in 1991, but that the New Zealand union wasn't keen and that this tour was a compromise. Some of my teammates had been on the All Black tour the year before, guys such as Shane Howarth, Eroni Clarke, Lee Stensness, Jon Preston, John Mitchell, Liam Barry, Blair Larsen, Steve Gordon, Mark Allen

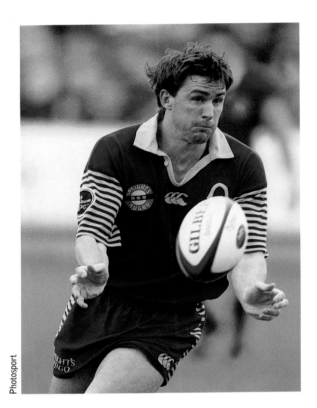

**John Leslie ...
undervalued nationally,
but never in Otago.**

and Norm Hewitt. There were other guys, such as Paul Cooke and Alama Ieremia, who were close to All Black selection (one made it and one didn't), others who were young and promising (Justin Marshall, Todd Blackadder), and some who must have counted their lucky stars that the national selectors had even noticed them.

I was pleased for Otago guys such as Cooke, John Leslie and Nick Moore because it represented a recognition for them that they didn't always get, either then or later. If I was to nominate the greatest errors of judgment made by any All Black selectors in the time I've been involved, among them would be their failure to give Leslie any sort of a chance beyond this one tour. He was a grossly undervalued player nationally, yet we in Otago knew not just how good he was as a player and as a thinker on the game, but how professional he was in his approach to it and what an influence for the good he was off the field. It was interesting how quickly Scotland, admittedly without the playing resources New Zealand has, snapped him up. And that was not just to play, but also to captain the side.

John Mitchell was chosen to captain the side in Argentina because he clearly had those difficult-to-define qualities that the best leaders always have and he had shown this in the difficult circumstances of the midweek games in Britain the year before. Though I doubt he was ever close to making the test team, he was an immensely proud All Black. I remember him the night of the game in Gateshead when players, changed into unidentifiable casual clothes, were scattered all over Gateshead and across the Tyne in Newcastle, unwinding as only rugby players can. Mitchell sat quietly at the bar in our hotel, still dressed in his No 1s. Asked why he hadn't changed and gone with his teammates, he replied simply and proudly: "I don't know if I'll get another chance to wear this gear so I'll just savour it while I can."

We're all proud of being All Blacks, no question of that, but Mitchell wore his pride on his sleeve. He was a good guy to be associated with and it was no surprise he turned down the extra money he was no doubt offered to stay helping coach England to return to New Zealand. If everyone had his attitude, there would be no fears about the future wellbeing of New Zealand rugby.

I wasn't all that thrilled with being on the tour and the longer it went, the less thrilled I was. I have no doubt I was included in the team in the first place

Photosport

John Mitchell, a natural leader doing one of the leader's chores, answering reporters' questions. The reporter on the right is Trevor McKewen, later to be the chief executive of the Auckland Warriors.

as a ploy by Laurie Mains to keep me firmly in rugby. There were still big question marks at the time, some in my mind and certainly many it seemed in the minds of the media and the public, about whether and when I would choose between rugby and cricket as my main sporting focus. It was increasingly obvious that I could not do both at the highest level and Mains' choosing me for the tour of Argentina seemed to me to be his way of tipping the scales in rugby's favour. He had said publicly after the Scottish test the year before, when asked what he could do to ensure I committed myself to rugby, that he was confident I was mature enough to make the correct decision in my own best interests. That was a very diplomatic reply. The selection to go to Argentina seemed to be his way of giving me a bit of a push to make sure the correct decision was rugby.

I think too that Mains thought I was still a bit fragile, mentally if not physically, as a result of my reaction to the loss to England at Twickenham. I suspect part of his plan with the Argentine tour was to see if some players, me included, could handle the rigours of such a tour. Rugby there can be very physical, especially in the forwards where thankfully I appear as little as I can get away with, and it can also be demanding off the field. Lots of little things combined on a rugby tour can upset a player's equilibrium and affect the way he plays or trains, and in Argentina there seem to be more little things than in other countries. The language is confusingly different, the food is different (though they have the biggest steaks available anywhere), eating hours are radically different, the attitude to rugby is quite different because it is a game based on the educated élite and very much a minor sport to soccer, and punctual is an English word that doesn't mean an awful lot in Argentina. Such things are sent to try New Zealand rugby players.

Our itinerary included two strong teams (a Rosario selection and the final match, a Buenos Aires selection) and the rest were fairly weak. But to say an Argentine club or regional team is weak is not to tell the whole story. What they lack in talent and skills they make up for with enthusiasm and many times it's enthusiasm that goes way beyond the bounds of the law under which we play. It's often excused as their Latin temperament. This was compounded by having local referees who were not all that experienced and who had to walk down the streets of their hometown the next day. I suppose the charitable thing to say is that playing a New Zealand team, even if it's not the All Blacks, was their big moment in the rugby sun and they went for it, boots and all. Sometimes literally. We were in their town two or three days and we were gone. They're there forever and forever will be judged on how they performed on their big day. So they made the most of it. We lost the two matches against the strong teams, and shouldn't have because we had more talent and knowledge than they did, but put the others away once we'd absorbed everything they threw at us and had worn them down with better constructive play and certainly better fitness.

I just wasn't happy to be there. It was the most poorly coached, poorly organised tour I've been on. Mains wasn't the coach, though he was the All Black coach at the time and was undoubtedly the boss, at least behind the scenes. He went there with the ludicrous title of assistant coach, which fooled no one. The designated coach was Lin Colling, who had been voted on to the national selection panel at the end of 1993 in place of Peter Thorburn. It must have been a difficult assignment for Colling, thrust into coaching a national team for the first time but with Mains there as well, it was only natural that he was looking over his shoulder all the time. I would have thought that New Zealand rugby would have learnt its lesson at the World Cup in 1991 about the folly of not having one coach in direct and total control.

I was left in no doubt personally that Mains was in charge because he climbed into me at one stage for what he called pissing about with the ball behind the posts. I can't remember the circumstances of the time,

Spot the assistant coach. Laurie Mains and Lin Colling.

but obviously I hadn't forced the ball as rapidly as he would have liked and he left me in no doubt about what he thought.

The happiest I was on the tour was when it ended and we flew home. If there'd been a cricket match to play, I would have gone and played it. While Mains may have thought going to Argentina would force me to choose rugby over cricket, it almost had the opposite effect.

The year didn't get a whole lot better. The first All Black trial was about a month after we got back but I didn't play in it and neither did any Otago or North Harbour players because we'd played in a national championship match the day before. That of course was nonsense. The trial was devalued because so many players were missing and it couldn't be called a true trial. That was when the NPC was scattered about the rugby season from April to October and it made focusing on it difficult for both players and spectators.

There was another trial in June and I played on the wing in that for the lesser team, the Possibles, which was a clear indication from the selectors that I wasn't being too seriously considered for the tests against France. And I wasn't. I was on the bench for both of those, watching the All Blacks lose games they should have won, especially the second at Eden Park when the French scored that improbable try that swept from one end of the field to the other. It was a magical try, no doubt about it, but the All Blacks should have stopped the movement. It was a case of the French expertise at making something out of nothing combining with errors of judgment, and even panic, among the All Blacks. But it's always easier to make the tackles from the bench than it is on the field.

Looking back now, the decision to not play me in those games was probably the right one and perhaps Mains knew more about me than I knew about myself, or at least as much. I think there was still a little fright in me from the year before at Twickenham, a little self-doubt about whether I could do the job. Those self-doubts would have been removed, or at least could have been, had I had more rugby because I would have had more recent experiences to gauge my form and mental state, but all I'd had were the unsatisfactory tour of Argentina — no guide at all — a couple of games for Otago and the trial. There's nothing like big games to get the confidence back up but I hadn't had enough of them. I was also going through a learning phase that all players go through, a harsh lesson that I was in the big time now and not everything would go as smoothly as it had when I was a supposed schoolboy star. Roy of the Rovers and Wonder Boy and all that stuff had been replaced by the pragmatism of reality.

South Africa arrived for their first tour of New Zealand since their isolation days ended and still I wasn't wanted, though I remained in the squad. I was just an interested and envious spectator when Mains started swapping things around, introducing Shane Howarth at fullback and putting

John Timu back on the wing in place of Jonah Lomu, who had been picked a bit too early though he was clearly, even then, a player of devastating promise. John Kirwan was on the other wing and there was therefore no room for me.

Mains never explained to me what he was doing or what his plans were, though he did say a couple of years later that his every move in 1994 was done with the World Cup in 1995 in mind, right down to the various moves in the game. He was criticised for that on the grounds that he was holding things back in tests for more distant goals, that he was even prepared to sacrifice a test to land the greater hope and glory of winning the World Cup. I have no doubt that Mains knew exactly what he was doing and why he was doing it all the time. One of the reasons we were such a good side in 1995 was because of the level of planning he put in during 1994. I have no doubt about that. Mains may have had his faults, which were exacerbated by journalists and broadcasters with whom he couldn't often get along, but his coaching expertise and his organisational skills should never be questioned. Technically, he was the best coach with whom I was associated.

That of course didn't help me at the time as I continued to train with the dirties and warm the bench during matches, watching the South African tests in Dunedin, Wellington and Auckland. Over those six weeks, I felt like a spare part and it literally drove me to drink. I'd never been a drinker but during the South African series, perhaps because I was so frustrated and not really feeling a part of the All Blacks, I started going out on my own at nights. Don't get me wrong. I didn't set out to drown my imagined sorrows or sit self-pityingly in a bar getting solace from a bottle (or in this case, a keg because I drank only Speight's). I'd just go out and have one or two quiet glasses on my own then rejoin the players in the team room at the hotel. I felt I had to get something out of being an All Black and of being with the team,

The reserves for the second test against France in 1994 – Norm Hewitt, Craig Dowd, Arran Pene, Graeme Bachop, Walter Little and myself.

Photosport

Photosport

John Kirwan in action against South Africa, his last series as an All Black.

and I certainly wasn't getting anything out of being on the bench.

Of course the dirties get all the peripheral jobs going, though that's not why they're called dirties. It could be though. I was duty boy more times than I care to remember, running around like an underpaid secretary ensuring players knew bus times and meal times, collecting laundry, loading bags on to and off buses — if there was a menial job to be done, I did it. The dirties also got lumbered with the extra tasks that face All Blacks wherever they are, such as visiting schools or hospitals, going to corporate promotions and other public relations exercises that players dislike but know it's all a part of the job. The difference those days was that the players didn't get paid for them (not legitimately anyway although we were, to use the euphemism, "looked after").

For me, the whole time was an enforced layoff even though I continued to train hard with the whole squad. But it's matches that you're a rugby player for, not training sessions.

It came as something of a surprise therefore that I was chosen for the Bledisloe Cup test in Sydney. It was more of a shock for John Kirwan, whom I replaced, and he responded to the team announcement by saying that Mains had lost the plot. Even for such a senior, respected player as "JK", that is not the way to earn your way back into the affections of the coach.

That match was an odd one, for more reasons than one. Mains was not at all happy that it was scheduled for a Wednesday night, the odd timing

Photosport

Shane Howarth in the 1994 test in Sydney, in which he was the All Blacks' only points-scorer.

chosen to avoid a clash with the televised opening ceremony from the Commonwealth Games in Victoria in Canada. It was odd for us as players too because test matches are supposed to be played at weekends or at least on Friday nights, but the adjustment in preparation was easy enough to make. If nothing else, modern rugby players have learned how to be adaptable. The only real disruption to our preparation was Robin Brooke still being troubled by injury and his enforced replacement by Mark Cooksley.

It became odder once the English referee, Ed Morrison, got it under way. His watch had barely started when David Knox kicked an up and under that came down on our line and Jason Little, as good as most Australians are with the ball in the air, scored. Such an early try seemed to set the tone for the first half and all we could do was hang in there, hoping things would change. They did in the second half and after Shane Howarth had scored midway through the spell, we knew we were doing enough to win.

I don't need any reminding that if I'd scored we would have won the game. I've been reminded about it almost every single week since and nothing in sport galls me more. Do people talk about how the All Blacks came back? No. Do people talk about how I beat three or four defenders to even get to the line? No. Do people ask how I scored this try or that try? No. All they can talk about, it seems, is how I was almost over the line when George Gregan pulled off a tackle of a lifetime and the ball shot forward out of my hands. That's the nature of sport. You win some, you lose some; the All Blacks win more than most. But what am I constantly, repetitively, boringly reminded about and asked about? That tackle.

I'm utterly sick of it.

What irks me most is these people who like to dwell on the things that went wrong rather than all the other things that went right. Perhaps it tells me more about them. What dull, dissatisfying lives they must lead if they can only ever look for the negatives, always talk about losses rather than victories, always talk about mistakes rather than things that have been done well and successfully. What is it in the New Zealand psyche that finds it so difficult to praise, yet so quick to condemn?

In answer to all those ghouls who like to live their lives on the black side of life, who find it so difficult to see good, yes I was devastated by not scoring. Wouldn't anyone be? Yes, I was upset. What the hell would they expect? That I danced for joy? Did I see Gregan coming? Yes, my peripheral vision picked him up but I thought I was there. In hindsight, would I do anything different? How can anyone answer that? Moments in a game are moments in a game. Things happen at blurred speed. Actions in high-level sport are often instinctive, not deliberate or calculated or premeditated. I didn't lose the ball deliberately in the tackle, you know.

John Walker went to Dunedin and talked to the Highlanders before the start of the Super 12 in 2000. He was a lesson to us all in the single-minded pursuit of victory, the need to rise above the mediocre, the pursuit of excellence. He told us he didn't dwell on his bad races, the races in which he performed below his expectations; they were history: he concentrated on the good.

It's a lesson for all New Zealanders, especially rugby followers who have

Tim Clayton/Sydney Morning Herald

Was I devastated?

Of course.

such high expectations of the All Blacks.

George Gregan and I have talked a few times since about the final moments of that match in 1994. He feels, like me, that it was one of the worst moments in his life, even though the result was good for his side. He's now expected to make tackles like that all the time and when he doesn't, he's asked why not.

George developed into a very fine player and the most dominant halfback in world rugby. He reads the game brilliantly, he's got all the skills, he rarely makes mistakes — his game is complete.

New Zealanders dwell too much on the bad times. They feel miserable when the All Blacks lose — and we had too much graphic evidence of that after the 1999 World Cup — and it's as if they want to know if the players feel miserable too. No, we feel a hell of a lot worse.

Was it as bad for you as it was for us? Worse.

That is the end of questions about that tackle.

# 6. The corporate world

One of the criticisms of the All Blacks after the World Cup in 1999 was that we had been "corporatised" and that we had lost sight of the real values of the game and were focused more on making money and living the lavish lifestyle than we were on preparing for and playing the games.

That's crap and anyone who knows anything about modern rugby knows that it's so.

It may be true that some members of the New Zealand union were concentrating on the money-making arm of the game (the Super 12 and the All Blacks) and sometimes they may have lost sight of the fact that 98 per cent of rugby in New Zealand is as amateur as it ever was — amateur in a financial sense. But to lay that on the players was grossly misleading and some who made the criticisms ought to have known better and perhaps some did, but still made the criticisms, anxious as they were to find something tangible, or what they thought was tangible, to explain away the loss.

It may be too that some people watched television commercials around the timing of the cup, particularly the National Bank commercial that featured myself, Taine Randell and Alama Ieremia, and thought they were real life rather than following a script and playing a role that was several hours of hard work. If that's the case, if people really did confuse a television commercial with reality, then all I can say is that they watch far too much television, have difficulty grasping reality and ought to get a life of their own.

I talk about the World Cup elsewhere, but the belief that All Blacks now are too "corporatised", implying that cellphones and laptops giving latest share fluctuations have become as much a part of our gear as mouthguards and boots, is just nonsense.

Rugby itself at the highest level is more "corporatised" — not a word that adequately describes anything and is too often used in a derogatory sense — because of the amount of money in the game. That's money that is invested by groups such as News Corporation, without which there would be no Super 12 and, perhaps, no All Blacks, and by sponsors. Theirs is the corporate world, not ours.

It affects our lives daily, but not in the sense that we strut about thinking we're tycoons in rugby boots. We're not. We're rugby players with the same or similar aspirations as all the rugby players who have gone before us and, in all probability, the same as all those who will follow. We prepare for games differently because of advances in training methods and video analysis and we play the games differently because the nature of the game has changed. But we're still just rugby players. We're athletes the same as those in any professional sport, the only distinction being that we play rugby.

We also do a lot more than train for or play rugby and it's one of the prices we pay for being professional athletes. I should emphasise this is not a complaint. We are aware of our responsibilities and of our obligations and we know what is required of us. We may not enjoy some of the things we're required to do, but does that make it different from any other job? I'm sure all "regular" jobs, no matter how enjoyable, have aspects to them that are not particularly enthralling but they still have to be done.

The advent of money for rugby players also greatly increased our workload. Everyone, it seems, wants a piece of the All Blacks or of the Super 12 teams and there seems to be a belief that since we're being paid, we have to be available for everything that's asked of us. If some of the players more in demand than others charged a reasonable hourly rate for their services, they would be earning much more money than they do now. Note that I used the word "earning", and not simply getting.

The more sponsors are signed up by the New Zealand union or by Super 12 teams or provincial unions, the more players are required to do. I believe the limit has been reached. The All Blacks have three main sponsors, News Corporation (which in effect means Sky since it bought the broadcast rights), adidas and Ford. They're three good sponsors and since they provide the bulk of the money that goes toward our earnings and the general funding of the game, I believe that our promotional activities should be confined to them.

Yet every sponsor, no matter the size of their sponsorship, seems to want almost as much as the big three want and that means more and more promotional work for the players.

The New Zealand union in particular went through a phase of signing up just about every sponsor it could, big and small, good and bad, and all carried All Black endorsement for their products and all wanted All Blacks to front their campaigns. Not only did it become far too time-consuming for the players, but I felt it also belittled the All Black brand. That brand is so powerful and vital for the wellbeing of New Zealand rugby, yet the level of sponsorship was such that it took it way out of the exclusive range. Wherever you turned, there were All Blacks endorsing this or endorsing that and the companies involved always wanted to use the high-profile players for promotions or advertising. But there is a limit both on time and on the number of players.

Perhaps one of the reasons for rugby's rush to money was that professionalism, and the consequential need to find extra revenue, was still new to rugby and the balance and value were being lost in the pursuit of extra cash. The All Black brand was not as exclusive as it once was. Sports that have been in the commercial marketplace for much longer have had more time and experience to appreciate the value of their prime brand and have priced it accordingly. Perhaps the best known is the five Olympic rings of the International Olympic Committee. It is one of the most valuable, if not the most valuable, brands in world sport and its use is rigidly controlled by the IOC. It is particularly fussy about which companies or groups it assigns the rights to use the rings. I believe the New Zealand union should use that as an example of the true appreciation of a sporting brand.

There have been signs over more recent months that the New Zealand union has realised it may have gone too far too soon and that it is now more particular about sponsors, and more conscious too of the commercial image of the All Blacks.

Servicing, if that's the right word, all the sponsors can be extremely time-consuming and counter-productive in the long term if our obligations to sponsors are going to start affecting the way we prepare for matches and, therefore, play them.

It is a particular problem for the All Blacks in Dunedin. If a company wants to make a commercial or do a photographic shoot, it invariably involves having to go to Auckland. What may be a three or four-hour job for an Auckland All Black turns into a two-day operation for an All Black from Otago, yet those involved in the organisation are too often not aware of that. Airline schedules being what they are, we catch an early-morning flight with a stopover in Christchurch or Wellington on the way, arriving in Auckland usually late morning. That means only the afternoon is available for the job and sometimes it goes on so long that it means an overnight stay in Auckland and therefore not getting back to Dunedin until something like lunchtime the next day. This is not pleasurable, luxurious jetting around the country, I can assure you. If such a job occurs during the 10 months of the year in which we're playing rugby, it interferes with our training and with other preparation for a game. If we've been injured, even a minor strain or something that doesn't prevent us playing, it means we are not doing the rehabilitation work that we should, to say nothing of the demands on the body of sitting in an aeroplane or standing around being photographed or filmed. I can understand why supermodels get paid so much and they don't even have to play rugby!

When such a job comes up and I suggest the film crew or photographer or whatever should come to Dunedin, cutting my workload from perhaps a day and a half to a few hours, every reason in the world is given why that can't happen. Too expensive, too many people, not the right equipment, not the right setting, not the right weather. "Aw, we'd have to stay the night and we have to be back in Auckland first thing." To that I say one word: "Tough." What about us, the supposed stars?

There has to be more give and take and I'm happy to say that the New Zealand union, which is usually the piggy in the middle in such situations, has grown to be more flexible and now better understands the players' point of view.

I'm not suggesting that we should be pampered or that we should have everything our own way. I'm not being a prima donna. What I am saying is that our value, whatever it may be, is as rugby players and consideration for that should come first because if that is devalued, so is the product we're endorsing.

And speaking about things being devalued, when will someone wake up to the fact that the more items — especially jerseys and balls — that are signed by players, the less valuable they will be? One afternoon a week at the Highlanders, we had a signing session and all the stuff was arrayed on tables and we had to sign each item. It never ceased to amaze me the amount of stuff that was dropped off at Carisbrook for signing. I imagine every other Super 12 team is the same. In 1999, we signed something like 2000 individual items during the course of the Super 12. We don't object to doing it because it's part and parcel of the job, but I do wonder about the value. It's getting to the stage that a ball or a jersey without the signatures of 26 or 30 players plus the management is going to be a whole lot more valuable than one with. For sale: limited edition pristine Highlanders jersey. No signatures. Only top offers accepted.

For the All Blacks, you can double or triple the number of signings.

These are quite apart from everything we sign as individuals — being stopped in the street or in restaurants or the autographs we sign after matches and, many times, after training. No player should object to signing autographs for kids, and few do. It is a vital part of the wider world of rugby. I can just imagine what would happen if some 11-year-old asked me for my autograph and I said "No, I can't be bothered." That kid then would grow up thinking All Blacks — or Highlanders — were a bunch of unco-operative, arrogant so-and-sos and he or she would be lost to rugby, perhaps forever. It takes nothing to smile, sign and say a couple of encouraging words, even if it happens 50 or more times a day. Whatever the effort, it's one that is well spent.

It used to be considered funny in the All Blacks and in some other teams for players to sign other players' names or, even worse, to sign names such as

Mickey Mouse or Donald Duck. That practice, thankfully, has died out. The value of the All Blacks is too high to engage in such childish, belittling activities.

A part of the price that high profile players willingly pay, usually willingly anyway, is the large number of promotional activities that have no commercial connotations as far as rugby is concerned. These include opening fairs, making appearances at a huge variety of functions, making speeches — all the sorts of things that go on in a community and that the organisers think would be enhanced by the appearance of a couple of rugby players.

The better known the player, the more the invitations. My father used to handle all the invitations to me and he was always very good at saying no, but at the same time being able to sense which ones were important and worthwhile and which were not. Some of the people doing the inviting used to be able to write exceptionally heartfelt pleading letters, but Dad was always able to sort them out. He had no compunction about saying no to the most heart-rending pleas.

No player should object to signing autographs after games. I certainly didn't, especially on this occasion because we'd just beaten Auckland.

I also point out that I have turned down many invitations, perhaps hundreds, that would have earned me money. Included among those were offers from various magazines or television programmes "to tell all" (or as much "all" as I felt I could tell). I did sell one story to a magazine, the one about my engagement to the Canadian rugby player, Sue Richard, but after that I just wasn't interested. Let the television stars wallow in it while they have the chance. I know some of the players have agreed to stories in women's magazines because at least that way they can control to a certain extent what is being made public about their private lives.

I have every possible sympathy for Jonah Lomu. The interest in him, by the public as well as the news media, is phenomenal and far, far greater than anything that happened to me. It's way beyond a rugby interest. He's even had a minder from time to time, and that's something no other rugby player has ever had. We've seldom been in situations where we've needed help. There is still some sense in the world. But Jonah gets hounded so much and so often that I believe it is that which will eventually drive him from the game.

Some people can get pretty miffed at being rebuffed. A woman phoned Dad once and said that her 12-year-old son was a great Jeff Wilson fan and could I show up at her son's birthday party. Dad immediately and politely said no, I couldn't or wouldn't. She then got abusive, saying that I was arrogant and stuck up and money-grabbing. It just confirmed to Dad that he was right to say no in the first place. There are some people who think that because rugby players are public figures, everyone has a right to a piece of them. They don't.

There are a great many invitations we get that we don't mind in the least accepting. School visits is one. All Blacks for years have been going to schools, whether in New Zealand or on tour somewhere, and long may it continue. It's fun talking to the kids and some of the players have got very adept at talking and they gradually turn it around so that it's the players drawing the kids out rather than the other way around. We're very conscious that it's from the kids at school that the All Blacks of tomorrow will come and, in much larger numbers, the supporters of tomorrow. Of course Josh Kronfeld is always a great favourite at schools, especially if he takes his harmonica with him. When he's asked if he's got it, he'll pretend that he hasn't, then a few minutes later he'll slowly pull it out of his pocket and the kids love him for it.

Another common invitation is to see people who are ill. I've been to Dunedin Hospital so often people must sometimes confuse me with Jeremy Stanley and think I'm part of the staff. There is a sad, poignant side to some of these visits. Some are to people who are dying and they just want to talk to a player before they die. It's especially sad if they're younger people.

They're the types of visits we never refuse. If we can bring some joy into what's left of their lives, we welcome the chance. Their attitudes in the face of death can be quite remarkable and there have been some times when I — and some pretty hard forwards — have walked out of hospitals or hospices with tears in our eyes. It puts life in a stark perspective. I think sometimes those types of visits can be of more benefit to the players than to the patients because they remind us of what really is important.

Just recently we invited into our dressing room a teenager who had been given only weeks to live. He was introduced to all the players and we sat around and chatted. His parents a couple of days later told us that it really perked him up and that night he'd been the happiest he'd been for months. We did little but if it helped him, even temporarily, so much the better.

I think I should state here that those types of visits, and many others that we do, are not "celebrity" visits. They are not photo opportunities, they are not done with a television crew scurrying along behind, they will not feature in a women's magazine the following week. They get no publicity, they are of no value in public relations terms for rugby or the individual player. They are done for the most basic humane reasons: someone wants help and if we can give it, we will. I don't want to sound like Mother Teresa here, but before we're rugby players we're just people and if whatever attributes we have can help someone less fortunate than us, we'll do it. It helps us as people as well as them. It can be a very humbling experience.

The "corporatisation" for me has included my long association with Nike, to whom I was contracted long before I was contracted to the Rugby Union or to anyone else. If ever my allegiance was in question, my first allegiance would be to them. That was put to the test in 1995 and 1996 when Josh Kronfeld, Ian Jones and I wore Nike boots for the All Blacks when we should have been, according to the Rugby Union, wearing Mizuno, which was then the official supplier.

When I was starting out, I wore Avia boots that my mother was able to get for me because of the sports store in which she worked in Invercargill. Then I had a short spell with Reebok when I was getting known in cricket. I wore Diadora, the Italian company that was then represented by the former Otago and All Black No 8, Gary Seear, in my first year in Otago but then David Howman secured me the contract with Nike. It was an employment contract, not just an endorsement one.

Nike and I fit like a glove (and yes, they make gloves!). They have a reputation as a bit of a rebel, the newcomer who didn't care too much for conventions and traditions, and they weren't afraid of a bit of in-your-face promotion. Their "Just do it" line sums up the company philosophy perfectly. It summed up mine too.

I spent a month in Auckland with Nike's New Zealand representative at

89

the time, Richard Reid — the hard-hitting international cricketer — and went to a Nike conference in Hawaii. My role was to promote their products and it was always a long-term plan that when I finished playing, I would work for them. They would have preferred me to be in Auckland rather than in Dunedin and in 1998 they made a serious proposal for me to move, but I turned it down. I wouldn't have felt comfortable there. But had I gone, it would have been to North Harbour, not Auckland. To their credit, they never put any pressure on me, just let me do what I wanted and keep doing it at my pace. It was an amicable relationship and I had the added bonus of having a contract that meant I could have transferred without any transfer fee being paid. I would have been moving because of my contract with Nike, not with rugby, and the Nike contract had prior claim because it was first.

It was partly out of loyalty to Nike, and partly out of a desire not to conform, that I chose to wear the Nike boots in the first test in France in 1995. Richard Reid suggested that I might wear them, but he didn't insist, as he could have. The decision was entirely mine. I was also perfectly entitled to wear Nike because this had been written into my NZRFU contract earlier in the year.

Among the people at the game in Toulouse was Jock Hobbs, the former All Black captain who was Mizuno's man in New Zealand. He was there doing comments for TV One's match coverage and he spied the boots instantly, as he would. The average spectator wouldn't have known or cared.

I must say that Nike didn't have the best rugby boots at that stage, but to me it was the principle of the thing. I'd talked to Josh and Ian Jones and we were confident we could wear the Nike boots without a problem. I should also add that while I had a contract with the New Zealand union, I hadn't been paid the $30,000 for the tour that the other players had been and in fact the money wasn't forthcoming for several months.

Hobbs complained to the All Black manager, Colin Meads, and he fired off a fax message to NZRFU headquarters in Wellington. Back came a fax saying I had to wear the authorised boots, Mizuno. I made my point to Meads but he, understandably, didn't want to get caught in the middle.

As it happened, I'd been injured in the Toulouse test and couldn't play in the following test, in Paris, so the issue went on the back burner.

I doubt that anyone thought of it again until the first test of the following year, against Western Samoa in Napier, when I again wore Nike. I was being loyal to Nike but, to be honest, I was doing a bit of stirring as well. Though it got mentioned in the news media, it never became a big issue because I think most journalists couldn't have cared less what I wore. But it was an issue for the union and for Nike and Mizuno.

The questions were fairly clear: Nike's view was that I could wear their boots because they had a contract with me. I agreed with them. The union's

Aspects of the corporate life. Wearing Nike in France in 1995 and note the blanked-out Steinlager logo on the jersey, done to satisfy the French government.

view was that I should wear Mizuno because the union had a contract with them that didn't allow exceptions. It came down to a question of commercial credibility for the union — how could it offer a sponsor exclusivity if it didn't then deliver?

Faxes continued to fly left, right and centre in the early part of the 1996 international season and I wasn't directly involved.

John Hart, who had taken over as coach, had inherited a problem he didn't want. "If you wear Nike," he told me," I can't do anything about it."

The ultimate sanction from the union's point of view was to order Hart not to pick me but neither he nor I wanted it to go that far. I had never wanted to jeopardise my availability for the All Blacks and that became the bottom line.

By the time we got to South Africa for the last of the tri-nations tests, the issue was resolved. I'm not sure of the details, and all I know was that I started wearing Mizuno boots for the All Blacks.

There were some slight echoes of that fuss the following year when the union was negotiating its new apparel contract with, as far as the public thought, the two protagonists, Canterbury International, suppliers to the All Blacks since 1924, and Nike. Neither I nor any players were consulted or involved, but I was kept in touch with what was going on and I was in a position to open a few doors. It came as a surprise to me, and I think to most people, when the new supplier was named as adidas, with both Canterbury and Mizuno thanked for their past services and sent on their way.

Part of the negotiating with adidas was an insistence by them that all players wore their gear, including boots.

They got their way even though in most international sports teams, or the big clubs of Europe and the United States, boots are seldom included in such contracts. They're such a crucial, personal item of sportswear that generally players choose their own. And a player being able to choose his own footwear also gives him an opportunity to negotiate his own contracts or endorsements.

The issue for a few months of what boots I wore was a battle no one was going to win, but it did give Nike some extra publicity.

The news media is a large and growing part of a rugby player's life. It has to be that way and no reasonable player would argue otherwise. And if they did, a very quick retort would be that if it wasn't for a news media company, News Corporation, we wouldn't be professionals playing in New Zealand. The media has always been a part of rugby, long before Murdoch's millions were introduced in 1995. The media is like politics and the weather, it's a part of daily life whether we like it or not.

Rugby gets the best media of any sport in New Zealand. Newspaper pages are full of it, radio thrives on it, television news bulletins would be lean without it and in terms of match coverage, television pays millions to get it. Without the media, rugby would be played in a vacuum. The news media in New Zealand reflects the intense interest there is in rugby. It reflects the good and the bad and if sometimes as players we don't like reading, hearing or seeing the bad, it's a fact of life and we just have to accept it. My advice to younger players now is that if they can't accept that and if they don't like what the news media says about them or about a game, then they shouldn't read newspapers or listen to the radio, especially talkback, or watch television. But there are plenty of players who say they never read the papers but you know that, secretly, they do. The lure of the name in print is powerful.

In my younger days, I got tired of what seemed endless demands for interviews. It got to the point that in an interview with the *Southland Times*, I said that if the incessant demands didn't ease up I'd have to seriously consider my future involvement in sport. I played sport for enjoyment and the satisfaction of achievement, not to fill newspapers or help the ratings of radio and television shows. I don't know that I would have carried out my threat but, with the help of a firm father, my comments had the desired effect and the demands eased for a while. There was also some reaction from the news media, one sports columnist pointing out that the media demands were a fact of sporting life and that I'd better get used to it. I may not have appreciated such advice at the time, but I certainly did get used to it. That is not the same as saying that I enjoyed it.

When I first moved to Dunedin and was living with my grandmother, Grace Robertson, she devised a novel way of deterring reporters on the phone. She had a cat that was ill and part of its therapy was to have its tummy rubbed. That was my job. Whenever a reporter phoned, my grandmother would answer and say: "I'm sorry, Jeffrey can't come to the phone because he's rubbing the cat's tummy."

The media demands have increased greatly since I have been involved and it must have been nice to have been an All Black in the 60s or earlier when the only media interest was from a couple of newspaper reporters and one radio broadcaster. Reporters, I've learned, were even allowed into All Black team meetings and rode on the team bus up until the late 70s. If that was still the case, we'd need to hire the Dunedin Town Hall for team meetings and have a fleet of buses — two for the team and management and half a dozen for the reporters and broadcasters.

It's not just a case of a reporter from a newspaper, one from a television channel and one from a radio station. Each has different departments or shows and all want their own material. I can recall being interviewed in a single day by three separate people from TV One, each for a different programme. From their perspective, of course, each is vitally important and each wants something different.

The former close relationship between players and reporters is just impractical now because of the sheer numbers involved and because of the diversity of the media. The news media, even in my time, has become more competitive and hungry for off-the-field stories, perhaps because of the increasingly powerful influence of television and the newspapers' perceived need to get something different.

Not all reporters or broadcasters want stories about who's going out with whom, in fact very few of them ask about that sort of stuff, but players are always wary whenever reporters or, especially, camera crews are around. There is a large barrier between players and the news media and that is partly because that's the way players want it and partly because that's the way the news media has made it.

Of course there are still reporters or broadcasters we get to know and think we can trust but because of the numbers, they're in the minority. When I say "trust", I don't mean that we tell them things that we know they'll never print or broadcast. We don't go that far and, in any case, there's not a lot to hide other than the obvious such as things that come under the broad heading of team strategies. By trust, I mean trust in their judgment and professionalism to get things right, even simple things like reporting interviews accurately, and to have a good knowledge and understanding of the game.

Quite often our judgment of individual members of the news media is formed not by how comments have been reported but by the depth or superficiality of their opinions. Sometimes a reporter might write that the Highlanders, or the All Blacks, played badly and were lucky to get away with a win when the reality may have been not that we played badly, but that the opposition were just better, either in terms of talent on the field or their game plan. It is not often that a reporter can look objectively at a game and analyse why certain things happen, or don't happen. Often their perspective of a match is influenced by their own expectations that come from the heart rather than the head, rather than by a rational analysis of the game. That is perfectly understandable.

There are reporters who, from time to time, get offside with players. I refuse to speak to one because years ago he wrote a story about my engagement to Sue Richard, yet never bothered to talk to me about it first. When I saw it in the paper, I was furious and I went to the editor and told him so. To me, such reporting was irresponsible and an invasion of my privacy. There is a place for such stories, but surely common courtesy, not to mention journalistic ethics, would dictate that the subject of them be at least given an opportunity to respond.

I was similarly furious when the "Jeff Wilson is gay" rumours raced around the country, getting to an absurd stage. At one point, a television reporter phoned the Highlanders and asked where and at what time the Wilson press conference was. What press conference? "We have it from a good source that he is coming out, announcing that he is gay."

If I'd been having a press conference, all I would have been announcing was that I was angry. I was especially furious when I was confronted by a reporter from a women's magazine at Christchurch airport when we were on our way back from the Super 12 semifinal in Cape Town. She approached me at the airport and asked about the rumours. I laughed them off, saying I wasn't interested in such a story.

I then went up to the Koru lounge and phoned my mother, to learn that the same reporter had been badgering her about whether I was gay. That did it.

I went back downstairs, found the reporter and gave her a bollocking in language that could not be described as gentlemanly. I might be fair game for the news media, and I grudgingly accept that, but it goes way too far when my mother or anyone in my family is involved. If she thought I was brutal toward her, she should be thankful my father wasn't still alive.

A couple of days later, we had an hour for the media at Carisbrook three days out from the Super 12 final. It was all the usual rugby stuff — "How do you think you'll go?", "Do you think the travelling will have an effect?" etc etc — but a reporter from *Sunday News* asked me about the gay rumour.

It was at that point my lawyer, David Howman, got involved and said that if anyone printed or broadcast the rumour, they would be sued for defamation.

Friend and lawyer David Howman.

He assured me that news organisations fully understood the defamation law and that should have been an end to it because they wouldn't print anything for fear of running up hefty legal bills. To my surprise, *Rugby News* reported the rumour about me and a separate one about John Hart. It did so in a misguided effort to dispel them but reporting the rumours was defamatory, no matter the intent behind it, and we had no choice but to take action. The settlement amounts we received went to the Burwood Hospital, where spinal and burn injuries are treated.

After that, the rumours thankfully died. And how did they begin in the first place? Who knows? What I do know is that in this case there was no fire, and definitely no smoke. My mother and sister-in-law had a great laugh about me being gay, recalling me on the sofa in younger days with various girlfriends.

There had of course been similar rumours about other

Howman Collection

prominent sportsmen. Since the advent of the Internet, there have been a number of false rumours, and I would hope that appropriate steps can be taken against those responsible. People can have whatever sex life they choose, and do whatever else they want, but it's pretty low if they feel they have to start a whisper campaign against someone else to justify their own tastes.

While the gay rumour was easy to laugh off because it was so far-fetched, it was also hurtful. I don't imagine anyone likes having their private life bandied about the country, true or otherwise.

The timing of it all was particularly bad as well. At the time, I was just beginning a relationship with Adine Harper, the Otago and New Zealand netballer, so it's easy to imagine her looking a little askance when hearing the rumour. She told me later that several people phoned her and asked her if she'd heard the rumours and asked if they were true. It wasn't the most ideal circumstances in which to develop a relationship.

As players, we realise we have an obligation to the news media. We also know what we can say to reporters and we know what we can't. Mostly, the reporters know where the line is as well. I'm never going to publicly criticise one of my teammates, a referee, the administration of the game or, very often anyway, sledge an opposition team. But while I accept the obligation to front up for interviews, no matter how frequently and no matter how often I get asked the same questions, there is also an individual right to say no occasionally. Several All Blacks after the World Cup in 1999, stunned and disappointed by what we heard of the reaction to the semifinal loss to France, now refuse to speak to a particular broadcaster. The reason was that he took criticism way beyond the realms of objective and constructive to a personal level. As players, why should we do him a favour and help the ratings of his show when he has attacked us in such a personal way?

Radio's demands can be the most onerous of the lot because there are so many stations and all want their own interviews. They're almost always phone interviews — very seldom do we see the person we're talking to. And it happens that the phone interviews more often than not have to be at a time convenient to them, to fit into their work hours, rather than convenient to us.

Radio also has talkback and if any player wants to retain his sanity and his confidence, he'd do well not to listen. Everyone is entitled to an opinion of course, but where I have a problem is that too many opinions are based on just a passing acquaintance with the facts, or are merely half-baked theories or, even worse, rumours with no basis of fact. Radio has a built-in delay to prevent abusive or obscene calls getting on air. Perhaps that should be used sometimes to prevent falsehoods, always assuming that the talkback host (or his or her producer) has sufficient knowledge to separate fact from fiction. The danger of talkback radio, as compared with journalism, is that those who air their opinions do not generally have the experience and knowledge of journalists. I would doubt that any of the detractors of coaches such as John Hart or Laurie Mains had ever met either of them, had ever seen them coach a team at training or ever heard them speak to players. Yet their views, as personal and uninformed as they may be, get a nationwide audience. I shudder to think that people might actually believe a lot of the stuff they hear on radio talkback shows.

The All Blacks and each of the Super 12 teams, and some NPC teams as well, have had media liaison officials for some time. Such appointments existed in other countries before they were made in New Zealand, and the first for the All Blacks was Ric Salizzo, who did the job when Laurie Mains was coach, and the second was Jane Dent, under John Hart. I don't envy them their job in the slightest. It's their task to take all the interview requests and decide which can be filled and which can't. It's a good media liaison person who can filter them out so that not all are passed on to the players. They are a bit of the meat in the sandwich, not particularly liked by the reporters and broadcasters who have to go through them, and sometimes criticised by players for passing on too much. They're also there to advise coaches when to talk and when not, and sometimes what to say and what not. With some, that's probably an even more difficult part of their job than dealing with the players.

Inevitably, it's the supposed high-profile players who get all the requests. That's one of the reasons why access to the news media now has to be managed. If Jonah Lomu, to use an extreme example, was to meet every

The meat in the media sandwich ... Ric Salizzo and Jane Dent.

97

Andrew Mehrtens seems to be having a good time in this interview with John McBeth (left) of TVNZ and Grant Lilly of Air New Zealand after the Eden Park test against Australia.

Photosport

interview request over a 12-month period, he would have little time to train and even less time to himself.

In my earlier days, I was a victim of the media frenzy and others who have gone through it have been Christian Cullen and Tana Umaga.

Some players can handle media interviews better than others. One of the best, at All Black level, is Andrew Mehrtens and he seems to thrive on them. But others either don't like them or are simply not confident enough or articulate enough. That's another reason why the interviews are managed. It's pretty much an inviolate rule that no players are interviewed from two days out from a match and that's fairly generally understood. That's the time in which the players should start thinking solely of their job in the game and not be sidetracked by peripheral issues. Some players would handle interviews late in the week without a problem, but some wouldn't. We're all different mentally. One player was absolutely hopeless after interviews. He'd handle the interview itself fine, but then his mind would be a wreck because he'd be thinking back over what he said, wondering if he said what he meant to say, wondering how he'd be reported, and he'd grab the paper the next morning or have an ear fixed to the radio, much too anxious to give any thought to his role in the game.

Additionally, there are "rules" about interviewing that some players would not dare break. One involves props. They hate being interviewed about props they're going to oppose because they know there's a fair chance that in the game they'll have their words tossed back at them. It's unwise for one prop before a game to say he respects his opponent and it's just about suicidal to say he doesn't rate him.

"So you respect me, do you, you tub of lard? You'll respect me a hell of a lot more after this game." That's the sort of intellectual conversation props indulge in during the fray.

We once had related to us a story about a Hawke's Bay prop who was about to play against Scotland, who were then captained by Ian McLauchlan, known as Mighty Mouse. But the Bay prop, showing more nerve than nous, said before the game that he would "deal to Minnie Mouse".

The result was as painful for the Bay man as it was inevitable.

Brent Edwards of the Otago Daily Times gets the lowdown after the Highlanders beat the Cats in 2000.

I have to be frank and say that some of the interviewers are not good at what they do. Some ask questions that are just plain nonsense yet we have to answer as if they made perfect sense. Similarly, some ask questions that we've been asked hundreds of times before yet we have to answer as if they're fresh and new and entirely different. That is sometimes difficult.

Then we get a reporter who, for lack of anything else, says something like: "Jeff, talk us through that game . . ." or, "Jeff, talk us through that try . . ." I sometimes feel like responding: "Why? Didn't you see it?"

Sometimes I've been so bored with interviews that I get a bit devilish and see if I can start something. During 1999, I made an innocuous reference to wanting to play cricket again and, sure enough, that line was seized upon as if I was about to abruptly quit rugby and open the bowling with Chris Cairns.

On another occasion, I casually mentioned that I couldn't play forever — surely stating the obvious — and that was interpreted as me thinking of retirement.

Sometimes, reporters have delighted me. I was pleased that someone found out that Tony Brown and I were doing an art history course at Otago University and wrote a story about it. It was a pleasant change to be talking about something other than the previous game or the next game.

There have been times when I have felt sorry for reporters, even cringed to see on television or whatever the results of a story. This has most often been when a coach and sometimes a captain has talked about an upcoming game and tried to claim the underdog low ground. I think it's fine if coaches or captains are circumspect about what their chances are in their next game because lots of unforeseeable things can happen in a game, but they still have to retain some semblance of reality.

It's a nonsense to say beforehand, if the All Blacks are playing Italy or Tonga, for example, that we're wary of them and that we go into the game as the underdog because of this or that. It's rare, and I wish it was even rarer, that the All Blacks are underdogs going into any game other than those against Australia, South Africa, England and France. Realistically and historically, we should beat every other team every time we play them. Even against Australia, England and France, we have a much better record than they do. It's fair enough to say that we respect all our opponents, because we do, and that some are capable of causing an upset, but to play the silly game of being the underdog is just idiotic. Why shouldn't we say we think we're good enough to beat them well if we can do the things on the field that we've talked about and practised? I understand the bush psychology that's sometimes employed by coaches, laying the groundwork in case everything doesn't go right, but it's surely far better to be confident before a match than diffident. It's a fairly basic lesson and the Highlanders were reminded of it at the start of the 2000 season by that great athlete, John Walker, when he spoke to us.

"If you don't think you can win," he said, "you'll lose. And if you don't think you can win, why are you playing the game?"

It may be acceptable in some levels of sport or society to merely take part, but that's never been my way and it's not the All Black way. One of the criticisms of All Blacks in recent years is that we haven't been hard enough. I dispute that, as would anyone who has had to confront some of the fatties from the forwards. What is a more valid criticism, I feel, is that we sometimes have not been hard-nosed enough. We have downplayed our advantages to our cost.

7. Best, but second

Whenever any athlete comes toward the end of a career, there is always something that they will regret, no matter how distinguished the career, no matter how successful they may have been.

One regret, one disappointment, that I will carry with me for the rest of my life is that I was not part of an All Black team that won the World Cup. Of the four rugby World Cups there have been, the All Blacks won the first, never looked like winning the second, should have won the third and could have won the fourth.

But could have and should have are pretty useless phrases in a sportsman's vocabulary. No matter what the public may think or say, no one feels losses more deeply than the players themselves. It's they who train and practise, it's they who sacrifice other aspects of their lives for their aspirations in sport, it's they who are out in the middle playing the game and trying to play it the best way they know how.

Some losses are easier to bear than others, but none is pleasant. When you know the team collectively has played as well as it could and perhaps exceeded expectations, but was beaten by a better team, the loss is bearable. What is not bearable is knowing after a game that you as an individual could have prevented a loss. That is just misery.

I recall what Andy Haden said years after the 1978 test against Wales when he dived from a lineout in a theatrical, and fruitless, attempt to win a penalty. He said he would do it again because the ridicule and criticism he suffered was preferable to him walking into the dressing room after the game, looking into a mirror, and saying to himself, "You could have done something to win that game."

All sports people undoubtedly feel badly after a loss. The All Blacks feel them particularly keenly for a number of reasons — because of their own expectations, because of the weight of history behind them, because of who they are and what they represent in rugby, and because of the huge public expectations. Losses by other national teams can be accepted, losses by the All Blacks never.

The World Cup we should have won was in South Africa in 1995. We knew we were as well prepared as we could be, we were superbly fit, we had the right game plan, we had the right players and we had the right management. We thought we were the most complete team in South Africa and that seemed to be a general view.

But we lost.

We lost because of a processed chicken hamburger. How absurd is that? But it's true. Forget the stories about a mystery waitress called Suzie and forget the stories about bookmakers and gambling and us getting nobbled, forget who said what to whom and what was overheard and what was not. Forget all the intrigues and perverted theories.

I can believe only what I know. What I know is that until the Thursday before the final, we ate at our hotel in Johannesburg in the same dining room as other guests. For some reason, we had the Thursday lunch in a separate dining room, reserved just for us, and several of the team and management had hamburgers filled with processed chicken.

We went to the movies in the afternoon to see *Pulp Fiction* and, during it, Craig Dowd and I started to feel unwell. I told him I didn't feel great and that I would leave and he said he wasn't that great either and would come with me. As we were walking out of the theatre, other players joined us.

We had one of the hotel vans and headed back for the hotel. As soon as we arrived, Richard Loe shot out the door and started throwing up in the garden. I raced into the nearest open room and started doing the same.

I went to bed and didn't get out of it for 24 hours. I was in isolation. I was miserable. I didn't see anyone other than Loe, my roommate, and

With one of the great men of rugby, Sir Brian Lochore, our campaign manager in 1995.

Photosport

Mike Bowen, the doctor. Most other players were similarly affected.

On the eve of the World Cup final, the most important game in my rugby career to that time, I was either on the toilet or thinking of when I would next have to go to the toilet. The day before, I had felt as fit and as confident of my preparation as I ever had. But now, I was wasted.

The campaign manager, Brian Lochore, told me later that if the cup final had been on the Friday, we would not have had 15 fit players. On the Friday afternoon, most of the team went to a nearby park for a walk and some of the players just slumped on the grass, drained of energy. Lochore, Laurie Mains and Colin Meads even discussed the possibility of delaying the final until the Sunday, but decided it was impractical.

I didn't eat on the Friday and on the Saturday

morning, the morning of the match, all I had was soup and a bread roll.

What a way to prepare for the final! We were beaten before we took to the field. There was talk of us having played our final the week before in the semifinal against England, there was talk of us not having a Plan B to offset the South Africans' defence, there was talk of us being psyched out by the overt South African nationalism of the day, Nelson Mandela showing up in a Springbok jersey, the South African Airways Boeing 747 flying low over Ellis Park, that sort of thing. Maybe all those were elements in the defeat, but the fact is the superbly fit and organised Springboks played a team of All Blacks not ready for the final because many of them were ill and lacking strength.

That's not an excuse. It's a fact.

I thought then, and still do, that we did extraordinarily well to have been so competitive in the match, holding the South Africans and forcing the final into extra time. We went so close to winning when so many of us should still have been in bed.

The South African factor made the difference. Had it been France we'd been playing in the final, as it so nearly could have been, I believe that we could have won, as ill as we were. We were a much better team than they were in 1995 and they may have regarded, as they did in 1987 and in 1999, getting into the final as their great achievement. A final against France would not have had all the extra nationalism about it that South Africa brought.

But the facts are there, as unpalatable as they were.

I don't remember much detail about the game other than the fact I felt terribly weak. I just have the haziest memories. There was an air of disbelief

Peter Bush

It looks as if I was praying. Maybe I was. After I'd gone off in the World Cup final.

in the team that this had happened to them. I was running on empty and after I'd thrown up at halftime, Laurie Mains realised that I couldn't carry on.

It's as inevitable as it is pointless to wonder what might have happened had things been different. We had been getting better and better as a team and I have no doubt that but for the food poisoning, as we must assume it was, we would have won the World Cup.

But we didn't. There was deep disappointment at not winning, but also deep disappointment at not being able to show in the ultimate arena how good we really were.

I don't believe the semifinal against England the week before, when we crucified them and partly made up for the 1993 loss at Twickenham, was much of a factor. We prepared for that game as intensely as any test in which I've been involved, but the All Blacks then, and before and since, have played tests in successive weeks without any diminution of performance from one week to another.

The World Cup in 1995 remains a galling memory, one of the might-have-beens, and one that everyone involved will have to carry with them.

Everything had gone so well, not just the cup tournament itself but the planning and buildup over the previous year. I know Laurie Mains was criticised when he said that he held some things back during tests in 1994 because he didn't want to show his cup hand too early, but it was flawless planning. The criticism was based on the premise that he had been prepared to sacrifice tests in 1994 for the greater glory of 1995, but I don't believe that was the case. Every test is important to the All Blacks and we want to win them all. What Mains did was to put the experiences of 1994 to a greater use in 1995.

The camps we had over the summer of 1994-95, starting with a general sort of brainstorming session in Queenstown, were all worthwhile and had the effect of confirming in all players' minds precisely what was required of us during the World Cup. Mains was also very particular about choosing players he felt were best suited to the way he wanted us to play the game. Too often coaches can go the other way: pick a team then impose a gameplan. It's much better to choose the game-plan first, then pick the players capable of executing it.

Planning from levels other than coaching was also ideal. One example of this was the appointment of Brian Lochore as the campaign manager. Initially, he had been appointed for just the New Zealand phase of the buildup but it was always obvious to us that he would be a crucial member of the team in South Africa. He was the sort of godfather to the team, ideally complementing the roles of Laurie Mains and the manager, Colin Meads. He also brought with him a different emotional perspective and, it should go without saying, he had the utmost respect of everyone in the team. His

Laurie Mains with two of the brains in the backs, Andrew Mehrtens and Frank Bunce.

personal manner was such that he never intruded into the roles of Laurie or Colin, but was always a great help to both of them and to the players. He also took a lot of pressure off Laurie for some of the public aspects of the job. I don't think I'm doing a disservice to Laurie by saying he wasn't all that comfortable with the news media. He never had an easy rapport with journalists, not even the regular rugby ones whom he knew well, and he always had a slight — and sometimes not so slight — suspicion that their interests were not the same as the team's interests.

Laurie is a very intense person, the more so when test matches approached, and Brian was able to relieve Laurie of many of the jobs that were peripheral to his main task of coaching the team and preparing us in the best way he knew how. His presence allowed Laurie to focus on the one single goal of winning the World Cup. Brian had an affable manner with journalists and it helped too that they mostly respected him as much as the players did. It takes a bold, and stupid, person to rile Brian Lochore.

Meads was Meads. What else do you say? He didn't have to say anything. He just had to be there. The whole world respected that man. I know the players were more conscious than usual about the value of the All Black jersey and of not compromising standards when he was there. We couldn't let him down. He'd walk into a room or into a restaurant and he just had this presence that made us feel like schoolboys in the presence of the principal.

Meads also whistled. Sometimes he'd wander round whistling some indeterminate tune to himself and we knew that when he did that, something was worrying him. That was the time to steer clear of him, just in case you became the target of his wrath.

Meads was Meads. The great Pinetree.

He would talk to us every so often about playing in his day or tours in his day when things were so different, but he wasn't the type who'd want to claim that things were better in his day. Just different. He and Brian both understood how much had changed and it was a benefit to the players, conscious of the All Black heritage, that we had two living examples of it with us.

I'd never been involved with Laurie Mains in Otago because he was already coaching the All Blacks when I moved to Dunedin, so I only knew him as a national coach in the more demanding atmosphere of the All Blacks.

The first time I'd had anything to do with him over a sustained period of time was on the tour

of England and Scotland in 1993 when I was the "baby" of the team and knew my place. I didn't quite call him "Mr Mains", but it must have got close at times.

I think I was probably lucky on that tour that he'd picked the young Auckland lock, Richard Fromont, who, deliberately or otherwise, became quite a target for Laurie. "Dicko" was a bit of a character in the team and had what might be called a laid-back approach to being an All Black, though he was serious enough in his rugby intentions. It was just that he didn't pay too much attention to some of the finer points of the discipline of being an All Black — things like wearing the right clothes at the required times, having shirts tucked in, or arriving at team meetings or other events on time.

Fromont thus drew himself to Laurie's attention more than other players and when Laurie admonished him for some minor misdeed, Fromont took Laurie head-on, which came into the category of red rag to a bull. Fromont as a result became a target of Mains at training as well and we'd hear commands barked out like, "Come on Richard, you're an All Black now" or "Richard, you can do better than that."

If Fromont hadn't have been there, I'm sure I would have been the target of such unwanted attention.

Richard Fromont during a trip to the Ferrari car plant near Bologna in 1995.

107

Photosport

Heading for one of three against Japan in Bloemfontein.

A lot of it of course was bark rather than bite and when Robin Brooke's fitness was in question during the early matches of the 1995 World Cup, it was to Fromont that Mains turned for a standby player. Fromont went to South Africa but under the cup rules couldn't join the squad until or unless Brooke left it, so he had a few days in South Africa at New Zealand's expense without having to do anything to earn it.

Fromont and Mains were almost friends by the end of Mains' career as All Black coach. For Mains' last test, against France in Paris, Fromont was among the dirty dirties — the players who sit in the stand — and was thus wearing his No 1s of All Black blazer, white shirt and tie and best trousers. In the general celebrations and hilarity in the dressing room after the match at the Parc des Princes, Fromont "fell" into one of the players' baths. Sopping wet, he was deputed by Mains to stand guard at the dressing room door to stop unwanted visitors (particularly the hordes of French journalists who seem to treat dressing rooms as their own workrooms).

AFL-style – and I got the mark ahead of the Irish fullback, Jim Staples.

I didn't entirely escape the Mains wrath. He rounded on me once in Argentina in 1994 and he did so again — silently — at the World Cup in

South Africa, after I'd played against Scotland at fullback for the All Blacks for the first time. I'd missed a couple of tackles though I didn't think I'd played too badly, but Laurie made it plain he wasn't satisfied.

He put me at first five-eighth at training the next day and had the forwards running off rucks and mauls at me. He didn't have to say anything. His actions illustrated his displeasure and all the other players knew I was being punished for what Mains saw as a sub-par performance.

That was quite often the way he worked. He'd make examples. He'd berate another player in front of the team, or he'd put a player through a particularly punishing training routine, and everyone else would know that it was directed at them as well, that there but for the grace of God went they.

Mains was a tough Southern Man, both physically and in his attitude. He

My first game at fullback for the All Blacks was in the quarterfinal against Scotland. I seem to have headed off Graham Shiel in this contest.

Will Carling gets me in the semifinal, but I get the pass away – I think.

Photosport

Laurie Mains ... he did everything possible to win the World Cup.

trained us hard and I don't think I worked as hard under any coach as I did under him in 1995. He was fair though, and there was never any chance of him playing favourites among players the way some coaches have done. We were all treated the same and Mains distanced himself from the players so that he wouldn't get close — or be seen to be getting close — to any players. He was criticised at times for picking Otago players, but I know for a fact that he was just as hard on them as he was on everyone else.

Most players were wary of him and we kept our distance as well and it was perhaps fortunate that we had guys such as Sean Fitzpatrick and Zinzan

Brooke who were tough-minded individuals and who would stand up to him if they felt the need. But even they were never close to him. There was an enormous lot of respect for Mains as a coach, but I don't think that ever extended to genuine friendship. Mains was single-minded in pursuit of what he wanted and God help anyone who stood in his way.

Not surprisingly, he relaxed considerably after he gave up the All Black job and he's much easier to talk to now. Of course it helps now too that he has no bearing on my life — I am not subject to his selection so it does make for an easier relationship.

Any coach of the All Blacks feels the burdens, and Laurie was no exception. He may have found it more difficult to bear the burdens than most because he was less able to relax than other coaches with whom I've been associated. It is a particularly demanding job. Not only are you coaching what's historically the best rugby team in the world and expected to maintain those standards, but you're constantly in the public eye. It's true that when the All Blacks win, the players get the credit but when they lose, the coach gets the blame.

There was no blaming of Mains after the 1995 World Cup. If there had, it would have been seriously misguided. He did everything he could have done to win the cup. The fact we didn't was through no fault or omission on his part. He ended up with a team that was the equal of the 1987 team that did win the cup. The only difference, other than in personnel, was that because of one lousy meal, we didn't.

It was, as I've said, a bitter memory that stays with us but, in the short term, it was a feeling of being let down by something we couldn't control, by having something within our grasp being snatched away from us through no fault of our own. I also think that the New Zealand public, unlike in 1999, were also still with us. They knew how good we were.

I suppose all the dramas of the World Rugby Corporation fuss soon after the cup diverted the general focus from one of disappointment to one of intrigue and, to those who were in the know, of deep concern about the future of New Zealand rugby.

Rugby players can't dwell too long on their losses or their disappointments because if they did, they'd end up with more of them. There's always another game to play, something else for which to prepare, and no one in top sport can afford to look back for too long.

What we had to refocus on was the two tests against Australia, the one in Auckland which we won convincingly enough, showing New Zealanders how we played in South Africa, and the other in Sydney, against the dual backdrop of the celebrations of the centenary test and of the WRC squabble reaching its climax.

There was too the National Provincial Championship which, from an

Otago point of view, provided another disappointment. We had a good team that was playing well, but we had a bitser of a season, losing to Auckland and Canterbury at Carisbrook and for a time looking as if we wouldn't make the semifinals. An away win against Counties helped us enormously but we followed that with a 24-60 thumping by North Harbour at home — so much for the much-touted theory that Otago are always difficult to beat at the beloved Carisbrook. We went back to Pukekohe for our semifinal and won that well enough, leaving the climax of the domestic year, the final at Eden Park.

That was the match, no Otago supporter should need reminding, that we should have won but didn't, a familiar enough theme for 1995. It's embedded in every Otago memory that we were leading 19-17 with just minutes to go when Stu Forster got over-anxious at a defensive scrum and Colin Hawke signalled the penalty try. It is not a pleasant memory. It's not pleasant either that I have yet to be in a winning Otago team at Eden Park. It's no consolation to say that a lot of other Otago players can say the same. Whisper it quietly, but it's a quarter of a century since Otago won an NPC match in Auckland.

Getting away from Mark Carter in the 1995 NPC final. Tony Brown is an interested spectator.

A long year, another disappointment, but still no time to look back. Time only to look forward. From being an amateur at Eden Park, I became a professional at a ground I'd never heard of before (and probably won't hear of again), the grandly named Santa Maria Goretti Stadium in Catania in Sicily. This was where the All Blacks' tour of Italy and France began, the tour that launched us firmly into a new era.

It was Laurie Mains' last tour as All Black coach and the first on which the All Blacks were fully paid for being rugby players although, to be precise, we were officially paid for being available for promotion rather than for playing. Since the International Rugby Board had just rubber-stamped the fait accompli that was the introduction of professionalism, our game in Catania against Italy A was the first legal professional game in world rugby. It brought with it implications that had not previously been a concern to the All Blacks. Only players who had signed contracts with the New Zealand union were eligible for the tour, even though some who had not had been playing fine rugby in the NPC and would, in former years, have been available for the tour. The intention behind it was to take only players who would be around the following year, but there have been many instances of

The fateful moment for Otago. Colin Hawke signals the penalty try that cost us the NPC title in 1995 while Marc Ellis pleads our case.

115

Josh Kronfeld makes his
nuclear testing point in
France, leg brace and all.

Photosport

players, knowing full well that they were retiring or moving somewhere, being chosen for the All Blacks. As a result, players such as Ant Strachan, Arran Pene, Jamie Joseph and Marc Ellis could not be chosen. It meant that, for possibly the first time, an All Black touring party was not chosen from all the best available players. It was an early cost of professionalism.

The match in Catania, in the shadow of Mt Etna, being the first professional game was the only reason to remember it. We didn't play all that well, even though the opposition wasn't up to much. It was one of those tour games that are now old-fashioned, one in which the opposition play for their moment of glory and in which the visiting team does enough to win and to survive for the following test. We achieved both. We won and we survived. One who didn't, though, was Andrew Mehrtens, who so badly damaged knee ligaments that his tour was over before it began.

Losing Mehrtens was a big blow. He has always been a phenomenal player and he's got better in the years since. When he's on top of his game, he's sensational and I like to tell him that he's far too intelligent for his own good. His brain is always going at a million miles an hour. What makes him so special as a player is that he's very hard to get to or to get at. He knows what he wants and how to get it and, generally, he'll talk anyone into submission.

Though we didn't know it at the time, we also didn't have the services of Josh Kronfeld on the tour. He was there all right, but hobbling along with an ankle injury that he sustained in the NPC final. It's well enough known now that he worked hard on his recovery, was ready to play in the match in Bayonne, then twisted the offending ankle again just before the game, and his tour was over. In hindsight, he probably shouldn't have gone at all but hindsight is a wonderful indulgence for people displaying their wisdom. At least being in France gave him a chance to fire a couple of bullets in the general direction of the Élysée Palace, criticising the French for continuing to test nuclear devices in the South Pacific. Several other players, as well as Laurie Mains, joined him in his political protest, but not me. I was a rugby player on a rugby tour, not a politician or a nuclear disarmament campaigner.

The tour gave us an insight into just what a phenomenon Jonah Lomu had become. We knew, naturally enough, that he was a star in New Zealand and South Africa but they're both rugby countries. What we didn't realise until we were in Italy was that Lomu's fame had transcended rugby and that he was a celebrity in a country where rugby is a minor sport and where the sporting idols are soccer players, cyclists or, in the case of Alberto Tomba, downhill skiers. Wherever we went, there'd be Lomu gazing at us from billboards or newsstands and outside each of our hotels or at match and training venues there'd be sometimes hundreds of people, mostly teenage girls, wanting his autograph or just to see him.

Italy and France in 1995 became the last of the old-style tours when

you'd play all manner of provincial or invitation teams midweek and, with only 26 players in the squad, back up for the Saturday matches which, on this tour, included three tests, one against Italy and two against France. With injuries having an impact (Tabai Matson, Carlos Spencer and Mark Cooksley all joined the tour as replacements), it meant a heavy workload for some players and, allied with the vast travel distances in France, it made for an arduous tour.

Playing in France is difficult enough without having added burdens. The French bring a peculiar brand of enthusiasm to their play which quite often takes little account of the laws of the game or, on occasions, of the morality of the game either. That's more an observation than a complaint because it's all a part of the diversity of international rugby, though the French are good enough rugby players that they shouldn't have to resort to dangerous and unnecessary practices such as eye-gouging and testicle-squeezing. Another example of how different the French can be was the way they prepared for the first test in Toulouse. They spent two or three days in negotiations with the French federation about how much they would be paid and, at one point, threatened not to play the test unless their demands were met. It's not the way All Blacks prepare for tests but it worked for the French because they

Getting away against Italy ... almost. Paolo Vaccari on the right may think he has me covered.

During the first test in Toulouse, not a particularly happy experience.

beat us, giving them three victories in a row over the All Blacks.

They lived offside in Toulouse and were allowed to get away with it, but we didn't play well enough to win anyway, our forwards in particular being dominated by the big French pack and life behind the scrum became a misery for Stu Forster (and led to the introduction of Justin Marshall a week later). What was most disappointing about the loss was that we didn't play anything like we had been all year and it was the one black mark against us (the World Cup final apart). It wasn't a particularly happy match for me either. I was at fullback, as I had been in the test in Italy because Mains was obviously dissatisfied with Glen Osborne's form, and had to leave the field early in the second half after I'd damaged a shoulder in a tackle.

That loss led to one of the great speeches by Colin Meads. Our next midweek match, in Nancy in north-eastern France, was sandwiched between the two tests and Meads in Nancy on the Sunday afternoon after Toulouse ripped into us, talking about the pride of the All Black jersey, the heritage that we carry, the fact that All Blacks should be held in awe by other sides and not be pushed around. It made a few of us shuffle our feet and look to the floor. We stayed in Nancy in a magnificent old hotel that was once a royal residence for Louis XV. The old courtiers of times gone by would never have heard such a right-royal dressing down as we received that day.

I don't know if it was significant, but Meads and the great All Black fullback of the 50s and 60s, Don Clarke, had sat deep in conversation in Toulouse the night of the loss.

Happily, though I played no part because of the shoulder injury, we were able to turn it around in Paris and at least give Laurie Mains a winning end to his four years as All Black coach.

8. A question of loyalty

As an athlete, you aspire to be the best. You practise and you play to that end and the further you go and the more you achieve, the more the other aspects of your life are subjugated to your sport. Your position as an athlete comes first and, sometimes at a cost, everything else comes second.

This is the way it has been for most of my life. I've been fortunate that I have had other people I've trusted to take care of peripheral issues so that my concentration on playing has been total. People such as my father Bill and lawyer David Howman and others were almost as crucial to the success I achieved as were my own efforts purely in the playing arena.

In the middle months of 1995, though, I found it increasingly difficult to concentrate solely on the playing of the game. This was at the time of the rugby war between the establishment game, for me represented by the New Zealand Rugby Football Union, and the World Rugby Corporation, the grand plan for a world-wide rugby troupe hatched by a former Australian prop and administrator, Ross Turnbull.

While I was able to leave the negotiating and the analysis up to David and to rely on him and Bill for the good advice I always received from them, the stakes were so high and the pressure was so great that, with the best will in the world, I couldn't totally divorce myself from the immense ramifications.

It's water that's long gone under the bridge now, but it's worth restating just what was at stake here. There was the very real prospect of most of the All Blacks World Cup squad of 1995 turning their backs on New Zealand rugby and the All Blacks forever. And the same in Australia, South Africa and other rugby countries. The world's leading players were on the brink of leaving the establishment game to play in Turnbull's WRC.

It would not have meant the end of rugby, neither would it have meant the end of All Black rugby because players can be replaced, as we are only too well aware. But if Turnbull's plans had succeeded, rugby world-wide would have been dealt a devastating blow.

And I was caught in the middle of it. I was confused, worried, apprehensive.

I was a relatively junior All Black then and not privy to much of the comings and goings or the whispered conversations between players and people in suits who were either rugby administrators or lawyers or sometimes both. There was confusion at times too about which side some people were favouring. It's not just horserace punters who have a flutter of a bob each way. There are some people today whose consciences would not stand up to even a cursory examination.

The rugby war of 1995 was an intense, intriguing time. But first some background. Rugby had been heading toward professional status for the top-level players since before the first World Cup in 1987. It was inevitable and players knew that it was just a matter of time. Players could not continue in an amateur world, losing money by taking time off work or not being able to work at all, while rugby unions became richer and richer through the distribution of television rights money and commercial agreements. The World Cup had provided the climate for increased haste toward professionalism; the WRC controversy provided the catalyst.

The advent in early 1995 of Super League in Australian league brought the whole thing to a head. The fight between Super League and the Australian Rugby League alarmed rugby because rugby players were ripe for the picking. Earn nothing from rugby or go to league and earn hundreds of thousands, perhaps millions. That was the choice and rugby bosses knew that it was a Hobson's choice, no choice at all. So they went searching for their own financial salvation and found it, ironically enough, with Rupert Murdoch's News Corporation, the same company that had bankrolled Super

Rupert Murdoch's money trail, as seen by cartoonist Jim Hubbard.

League. They struck a deal in which News would finance southern hemisphere rugby for 10 years in return for sole television rights to the domestic and international programmes in New Zealand, Australia and South Africa. The deal included the introduction of the tri-nations and of what was then known as the International Provincial Competition, which later became known as the Super 12. The broad details of the arrangement, on the face of it a magnificent deal for rugby, were made public on the eve of the World Cup final in Johannesburg. I don't recall even noticing it at the time. I was more concerned with negotiating my way from my bed to the toilet and back again, wondering if I would be able to play in the cup final the following day.

Behind the scenes, and I was totally oblivious, counter forces were at work. Turnbull and his colleagues dreamt up their plans for the WRC, which would have involved quasi-national teams playing each other around the world — not necessarily in rugby-playing countries — in a scheme that seemed similar to the Kerry Packer cricket series at the time of that game's great rift in the late 1970s. Some All Blacks, I later discovered, were privy to these plans but I wasn't. In the early stages, they were confined to just a few senior All Blacks.

What was going on became clearer when we were back in New Zealand and after a parliamentary reception in Wellington, we went to a hotel near the airport where we were addressed by the chairman of the New Zealand union, Richie Guy. He outlined to us what the New Zealand union proposed to pay players now that it had its News windfall, but I got the impression that not many of my teammates were giving him their full and undivided attention. The reason became obvious. What he was offering was much less than what WRC was offering. Led by the senior All Blacks, we left the meeting, knowing we were taking a first step against more than 100 years of rugby tradition.

The NZRFU chairman in 1995, Richie Guy.

I frankly admit that I signed a letter of intent with WRC and later, a contract. For the signing itself, I would receive $100,000, the same signing-on fee promised to every player. Sufficient money to cover the signings had been deposited in an Auckland account administered by an Auckland law firm. The money was in the bank. I would be paid $100,000 for signing my name. If WRC had gone ahead, I would have been paid somewhere between $700,000 and $800,000. That was more than some players were offered, less than others. (For the record, I did not receive the $100,000 signing-on fee. Some All Blacks pursued its payment through the courts, but I was not among them.)

It was an exciting time. It has to be understood that the All Blacks had been together for a couple of months and it was a comfortable environment in which to be. We trusted each other in our close-knit community and it was easy to go with the flow. To sign was an easy decision to make from the inside. We trusted the views of people such as Sean Fitzpatrick, Zinzan Brooke and Mike Brewer and others who had been around the All Blacks for longer. Looking from the outside, which I did not have the luxury of doing, would have brought an entirely different complexion to it.

Others, of course, were looking entirely from the outside and did not like

123

what they saw. It was only as the whole thing gained momentum that I could see what those on the outside were seeing and that the ramifications went far wider than I had appreciated.

I don't think I was particularly naïve at the time or that I was led by the nose into doing something that I would later regret. They were confusing times as well as being exciting and I was thankful that I had people like my father and David Howman who could look at it all much more objectively and from the outside.

Faced with similar circumstances today, when I'm older and wiser and a senior All Black, I would never sign for a body like the WRC.

Things reached a head the weekend of the Bledisloe Cup match in Sydney. It was supposed to be a weekend of celebration of 100 tests between New Zealand and Australia, a time of reliving past glories and revelling in the rich history of rugby between the two countries. Instead, it was a time of even more intense intrigue.

There was speculation that Josh Kronfeld had been left out of the team to play in Sydney because he had not signed the letter of intent with WRC. Neither he nor I know why he was left out, but he was.

I was focused totally on the rugby because it was a test match and because it was my first match in Sydney since the dreaded George Gregan match there the year before. I wanted redemption. That was what was on my mind, not the competing forces for rugby's soul. My needs were much simpler. I wanted the All Blacks to win and I wanted to contribute in the best way I knew how to that win. The All Blacks did win and I scored a try and played, I felt, reasonably well. All that was forgotten, though, in the aftermath.

New Zealand and Australian newspapers that morning had news of the potential split in rugby and it was surprising really that it had all been kept out of the news media for so long. The confirmation for the public that something was amiss came immediately after the test. Post-match comments are usually bland and banal, words strung together but saying nothing. The words at the Sydney Football Stadium were dynamite.

The president of the Australian Rugby Union, Phil Harry, stood and said: "This is the end of the season and in many ways is the end of an era. Let me say this . . . that sort of spectacular, passionate game between two nations is something that money can't buy."

Phil Kearns was the Australian captain and he then spoke: "To all Australian supporters here today, we thank you. It's been terrific, your support. And whatever happens in the future, we hope you and the union support us."

There, it was all out. There was much going on that I didn't know about. I didn't know that our campaign manager in South Africa, Brian Lochore, had been roused out of bed in the Wairarapa and sent to Sydney

A simple need satisfied:
scoring against Australia
in Sydney.

in an effort to stop the All Blacks from going to WRC. I didn't know that lawyers from near and afar were locked in talks in Sydney through the night and that some New Zealand union officials had missed half the game as they stayed in their hotel rooms working out how to save the game. I didn't know that they'd been working on a letter to be delivered to each of us, which read:

"We realise that you have been placed under tremendous pressure by the circumstances surrounding offers from both the NZRFU and WRC. We very much regret this, and we have endeavoured to reduce the pressure as much as possible. We are conscious of our duty towards you and the other 150,000 rugby players currently playing in New Zealand. We are also conscious that we must act responsibly so that all New Zealand rugby, including All Black rugby, continues to be strong and your sons have the same opportunity to wear the Silver Fern that you have had."

It was signed by Brian Lochore, Jock Hobbs and Rob Fisher. They were the three who had been deputed the job by the NZRFU of keeping the All Blacks within the fold.

The levels of intensity and intrigue increased after we'd changed at the Sydney Football Stadium and boarded the team bus. Instead of going back to our hotel or to where the test dinner was to be held, we meandered

Photosport

Laurie Mains and Sean Fitzpatrick in happier times than those that confronted us all midway through 1995.

through Sydney's classier area and the big bus manoeuvred down a tight crescent in Vaucluse, to the home, I discovered, of Brian Powers, a senior assistant of Kerry Packer. The reason for the visit was to demonstrate that Packer was indeed involved and that it was his money that was behind the WRC. We all trooped into the house except for our manager, Colin Meads, and coach, Laurie Mains, who stayed on the bus. Perhaps others of the management stayed on the bus too, I don't recall. One of the players, Anton Oliver, had to troop right back out again. The Sydney match had been his introduction to All Black rugby because of an injury to Norm Hewitt, but because he hadn't been involved all year, his presence was not required. While we sat in the opulent surroundings and listened to a pep talk on the merits of WRC, he played basketball outside with some of the house owner's kids. Among the talkers were Sean Fitzpatrick and Zinzan Brooke, who told us how good WRC would be for world rugby. It was on that visit that we signed. There were some who didn't. Marc Ellis was having his own negotiations and didn't pledge himself to WRC, and neither did Jonah Lomu. Ant Strachan had earlier committed himself to Japan and I suspect that Walter Little and Glen Osborne didn't sign either, though I'm not sure of that.

Mains evidently got increasingly agitated sitting out in the bus and poked his head in the door a couple of times, urging us to get moving. On his last visit, he told us we had to be at the test dinner and to arrive late would be a display of extremely bad manners. It struck me that it would have been even worse manners to enjoy the hospitality of the dinner, then tell our hosts we'd signed with the opposition.

Now that most of what was going on was out in the open, public feeling became polarised and heated. The atmosphere at the dinner, which was supposed to have been a joyful celebration, could have been cut with a knife. On the one hand there were players, New Zealanders and Australians, who were contemplating a wealthy future, and on the other were officials and former players who felt that we were stabbing them and the game in the back, disloyally trampling on all their traditions and pride.

We went home the following day to be confronted by headlines in the Sunday papers. *The Sunday News*, subtle as always, kept it brutally simple: "Packer bastards", it said. In the *Sunday Star*, David Kirk was more eloquent but no less damning. "To the older players and some coaches and administrators who are leading the charge to the WRC," he wrote, "I say 'go'. Get out, leave, remove the stain, the blot you are on the spirit of rugby. Take whatever money you can get, from whoever you can get it, but leave before you do any more damage."

It brought home to me very clearly the climate to which we had returned. Heroes one minute, pariahs the next.

I was already starting to have second thoughts. I don't think many of the players who signed truly understood the ramifications of the whole thing. I know I didn't and I was conscious that within the All Black environment, I was listening to only one side of the argument and did not have access to people such as Dad and David to whom I would normally turn. It's one thing listening to and trusting players such as Sean Fitzpatrick or Zinzan Brooke on rugby matters, it's quite another when the matters move beyond rugby. I was increasingly confused and worried.

David Howman and I knew each other well. He had first become my lawyer in 1992 when I was still in Invercargill and my father and Ian Donaldson, the chief executive of Sport Southland who had played rugby for Southland, decided that if I was to pursue a career in sport, I needed a lawyer who understood sport. Donaldson had met Howman at a Hillary Commission function and phoned him and asked him if he could go to Invercargill for a meeting. David went and met Bill, Ian and my mother, Lynne, and the partnership was born at that meeting, at which I wasn't even present.

David was also close friends with Richard Reid, who was then the Nike boss in New Zealand, and it was through that friendship that my association with Nike began. The triumvirate of my father, David Howman and Richard Reid had been beneficial to me in many ways over the years and it was to

Photosport

With international cricketer, friend and business colleague Richard Reid.

prove beneficial again in this time of rugby crisis.

David and a Dunedin lawyer, Warren Alcock, who acts for many players including Josh Kronfeld, had been studying the WRC setup and the way David explained it, he looked at the big picture and Warren was the details man. Both reached the same conclusion, that WRC was on shaky ground because it did not have guaranteed the vast sums of money it was committing itself to. The premise was that the money would be Packer's, but it would only be forthcoming once the players were signed, sealed and delivered. It had become much the same in the other camp, with Murdoch's company saying it had agreed to its package only on the basis of the top players being available and if they weren't, the money would be withdrawn.

The weeks following the match in Sydney were weeks of intense strain for the principal negotiators, especially the man who bore the brunt of the New Zealand union negotiating, Jock Hobbs. All involved had long days and long nights with constant phone calls and meetings, some of them in bizarre circumstances. David met Jock Hobbs once in what was known as the "war room" at the law firm of Kensington Swan in Wellington and rather than talk there, they walked along the road and sat on a pew in Old St Paul's. They weren't there to pray, but they may have dropped the odd plea to a higher authority.

David and Jock also met, on a Saturday afternoon, in a downtown Wellington bar called Paris. They met out the back, where they could be neither seen nor overheard.

Former All Black captain Jock Hobbs, who bore the brunt of keeping the All Blacks in the NZRFU fold.

Photosport

David told Jock that he might be able to deliver two All Blacks back to the fold. One was me, the other was Josh Kronfeld, David having been entrusted by Warren Alcock to act on his behalf.

After talking to Dad and David, I had left it entirely up to David to act in my best interests. My trust in him was total and I would do what he recommended. I had reached the stage where I was not comfortable with the WRC deal. It had become too plain that if WRC went ahead, there would be no current All Blacks. New Zealand rugby would have to start anew. I didn't want to be responsible for that. That was not a burden I wished to carry for the rest of my life. I was extremely conscious that the All Blacks had reached a "one in, all in" pact, but I felt that it had been reached in a false climate in which proper, detached advice had not been available and that all the negotiations to that point had been only by the players.

David and Richard Reid were able to play the Nike

card with the NZRFU, believing that if they could deliver me, as well as Josh who signed with Nike around that time, that would be of benefit to Nike when the New Zealand union's apparel contract was up for renewal. One of the ironies of the time (and there were many) was that the New Zealand union's principal negotiator, Jock Hobbs, was also the New Zealand agent for the NZRFU's boot supplier at the time, Mizuno, and its contract was also running out. This had ramifications later in the year and in 1996 when I wore the Nike boots in tests, much to the dismay and even anger of Jock and the New Zealand union.

Another irony was that when the apparel contract was eventually negotiated, Nike was a strong early contender but fell out of the running through no fault of any of the New Zealanders involved, especially Richard Reid, and the contract went instead to adidas.

David, Warren and others continued to work away with the NZRFU at varying levels while keeping close watch on what was going on with WRC in Australia and South Africa. It became increasingly evident that once the rugby establishments in the various countries got off the back foot they'd started on, WRC was losing ground. A particular blow to its aspirations was when the Springbok captain, François Pienaar, could not deliver the South African squad, which had fallen prey to the persuasive powers and financial muscle of Louis Luyt.

If the house of cards was being leaned on in other countries, it was Josh

Key figures at the South African end of things, Louis Luyt and François Pienaar.

Photosport

Photosport

and I who gave it a fatal push in New Zealand. David had been able to negotiate successfully with Jock on our behalf at the same time he and others were acting for a great many provincial players.

A press conference involving players such as Jon Preston from Wellington, Errol Brain from Counties and Stephen Bachop from Otago was being organised in Wellington. It was timed to coincide with an Otago team stopover at Wellington airport on the way to playing King Country in Te Kuiti.

David rang me and told me of the press conference, told me of the deal he had been able to do with the New Zealand union for Josh and me, and recommended that we sign as well.

I was then living in a flat not far from Josh and I jumped in the car and went and saw him. We sat around and discussed it, wondering what we should do. The All Black thing was a powerful magnet, more powerful than the money. Josh took the view that he had been an All Black in seven tests but he wanted to be a great All Black and play many more. My view was that if we didn't sign, there wouldn't be any All Blacks left. Without trying to sound like a martyr, we had the chance of saving the All Blacks. We knew that if we signed with New Zealand, others would follow and the WRC would be history.

We joined the rest of the Otago team on the flight to Wellington and, as we left the aircraft, met David on the lip of the airbridge. He didn't want us to go any further because there were too many ears and eyes — including the news media — in the old terminal building. So we sat and leaned on the airbridge and had our final discussions. David made it very plain to us what the deal was and warned us that if we signed with New Zealand, we would have 20 or so "enemies" among the rest of the All Blacks. We would not be flavour of the month with many of our teammates, but we would be hailed nationally as the first All Blacks to make the break from the WRC.

It was a momentous decision. But it was also an easy decision. Money matters aside, it was a question of ensuring the All Black tradition was not devalued. We owed it to ourselves to get the best deal possible, but we also owed it to New Zealand rugby generally and to the All Blacks in particular.

We agreed. David joined the press conference in the terminal with the other players and whispered in Jock's ear, "They've signed." It may have been the first time in weeks that Jock smiled.

Josh and I had had enough — we just wanted to play rugby.

I can't presume to speak for Josh, but I believe I made the decision that was best for me and for New Zealand rugby. One regret I had was that, in hindsight, I should have told the other All Blacks first. They deserved better than learning about my switch via television.

I learned later that some of the other All Blacks were also negotiating with

Together in times of strife, still together in times of joy.

131

the New Zealand union so the unity for WRC was not as tight as others thought it may have been and it wasn't just players who were having second thoughts. Others involved in the game swayed with the wind but kept their options to themselves.

There were some repercussions from other players. Zinzan Brooke made a half-joking comment about us being caught on the bottom of a ruck and others raised it in later conversations. I had a long talk once with Robin Brooke and Craig Dowd about what may have happened had WRC gone ahead and I think we agreed that, in the long term, everything had worked out fine.

Because Josh and I signed with New Zealand first, we got the first slice of the pie and we were probably better off than some who signed later. But it wasn't about money. That was never the prime consideration. I didn't grow up with money and money had never been the main motivating force in my life. During those frantic months of 1995, it wasn't the money that was the main factor. What they were asking us to do was to turn our backs on the All Blacks — and that we couldn't do. I think it was an unfair burden.

It was also wrong that the decisions potentially affecting the whole of New Zealand rugby were being made by one small group, the All Blacks themselves.

I was lucky that I had a lawyer and friend whom I trusted and believed in. Had I not had the guidance I had from David, Bill and Richard I don't know what would have happened. WRC may have gone ahead. No one can know. I probably would have made the same decision as the other players.

All Black rugby, New Zealand rugby, would have changed forever. It did change as the result of WRC, but not in the way it would if we had gone ahead with it.

The All Blacks, within the national consciousness and within world rugby, are a powerful, enduring force. Whatever my contribution, I can rest easy that I did not contribute to a diminution of that.

9. A year in the sun

It is very seldom that I feel sorry for opponents. Why should I? Any game is there to be won and the greater the victory, usually the greater the satisfaction at a job well done. If opponents get dispirited, that's their problem. If they want to take us on, they've got to accept what they get, just as we do if we lose.

But I had to admit to a slight feeling for Western Samoa after the first test of 1996. Everything was in our favour and very little in theirs. The night match in Napier marked the beginning of a new era for New Zealand rugby and for the All Blacks and we were excited by it. There was a real buzz within the team as if we collectively felt that we were in the vanguard of something really special. With that sort of attitude in the New Zealand camp, the Samoans didn't have a show. We beat them well enough, 51-10, and never felt that we didn't have the game under control, but All Blacks are never truly satisfied — or at least shouldn't be — and we made enough mistakes to give us plenty to think about for the tests ahead.

The Samoans caught us at a bad time: bad for them, good for us.

The dramas of the previous year now behind, 1996 was the first year of the new rugby and I know players were excited by it and there was plenty of evidence that the public was too. Everything, it seemed, had changed except for the shape of the ball and no matter that we'd played through to the end of November in 1995, the novelty aspects of 1996 ensured that we were fresh and enthusiastic.

The Super 12 had been a roaring success and the three new partner unions, New Zealand, Australia and South Africa, were fortunate that they'd had the previous experience of the Super Six and the Super 10 — and, in the case of Otago and some others, the CANZ series. That experience meant the organisation of an early-season competition didn't start from scratch and because New Zealand players were so familiar with each other, the draft system was no disruption at all. We were all professional players, living and breathing rugby day in and day out and it was all still so refreshingly different that problems associated with constant rugby were still in the future.

Being professional and contracted to the New Zealand union, we played

where we were put but that wasn't a problem either, especially not in the Otago Highlanders which was essentially Otago under a different name and in a different jersey. Carisbrook was still our home; we merely transferred the Otago way of doing things from one team name to another.

I was excited at playing test players week in and week out in the Super 12 and what makes it so hard now, the constant grind of weekly matches, nearly all of which are critical, was a novelty then so the burden was borne more lightly.

My attitude was also helped by playing in the Shell Trophy over the summer on the basis that a change is as good as a holiday. It was good to be back with the cricket boys for five games — nine innings for an average of 34.66 and 15 wickets at 35.26 if you must know. It's such a different environment and rugby was happy to let me do it, reasoning that it would do me more good than harm. I played well into February which meant that I missed much of the early buildup phase to the Super 12, though I had no qualms about my fitness.

It was a year of hugely significant change in New Zealand rugby and it was great to be a part of it. Among the changes was the introduction of John Hart as All Black coach, who had secured at the end of 1995 the job he had always coveted. Players are always a little apprehensive about a new coach because they don't know if he'll have the same regard for the same players as his predecessor and because there's always a settling-down period as he gets used to the players and they to him, and everyone gets used to new ways of doing things.

Rugby philosophies may be similar, as they have been with most of the coaches with whom I've been involved, but there are always new ways of translating philosophies into practice. John Hart and Laurie Mains, for all their public bickering, were very similar in their approach to rugby, though they had vastly different personalities. I didn't know that then though.

I'd met Hart on a few occasions, usually when I was with the All Blacks and he was doing television comments. I'd never had any long conversations with him but he was friendly enough and there was never any doubting his passion for rugby and the All Blacks. I knew of his record as a successful coach of Auckland, though not in any detail because I'm not a great student of statistics, and I also knew the broad outline of his background as a New Zealand selector, as coach of the Colts and as co-coach at the World Cup in 1991. I wasn't involved in that cup of course, but I'm sure any player then, as now, would have known that a co-coach system just cannot work. There has to be a boss who stands or falls by his decisions.

Clearly, Hart was going to make a mark as coach of the All Blacks and, in many ways, he was the ideal person to be the first professional coach. His experience as a senior executive with Fletcher Challenge fitted him well for

The new era brought a new competition, the Super 12. This was against the Auckland Blues at Pukekohe.

135

John Hart has my full attention at halftime in Durban in 1996. Below: All Black manager from 1996 to 1999, Mike Banks.

dealing with all the peripheral issues that came with the professional game, and he was always a meticulous planner and organiser. Professional rugby demanded a new approach to team organisation and John Hart, along with manager Mike Banks, who was a successful businessman, provided it. For all the changes, the most obvious was that we were under contract and being paid, but a significant change, and one which may not have been appreciated by everyone at the time, was that we were much more accountable than All Blacks had ever been before. In the earlier days and until 1995, players were amateur and though some over recent years had been able legitimately to earn money through promotions and commercials, we were all still essentially amateur in the financial sense of the word. Professionals in attitude, amateurs in payment. That was us. Implicit in that status was that we were free agents. We could play when we wanted, and not play when we didn't. We could be available for one tour, but not for another.

That changed forever in 1996. We became accountable to our team, the union and, indirectly, to the public. We were judged, as All Blacks forever have been judged, on our performances but now we were playing not only for pleasure or pride, and we certainly still played for that, but also for our livelihood. The International Rugby Board's decision to make the game "open", as predictable and as catching up with the reality as it was, altered the dynamics of rugby forever. Many of the implications of that decision were not to be realised for some time and I know I, and I'm sure most players, was just happy to be being paid for something I enjoyed doing and would have continued to do anyway.

In those early months of 1996, even though Hart was doing all the planning, I still didn't have much contact with him because Gordon Hunter was also on the national selection panel and, as the Highlanders coach, he was the obvious first point of contact. Also, during that period there was so much that was new and different with the Super 12 that I didn't think too far ahead to the All Black season, which brought with it the tantalising prospect of the first tri-nations series followed by a separate tour of South Africa.

That all changed when we came together in Hawke's Bay for a trial match in Napier with the test against Samoa the following week. Most of the All Blacks, plus some who were soon expected to be, had already had a couple of weekends of seminars and get-togethers where the plans for the year were spelt out and when the importance of being All Blacks, and the responsibilities that go with it, were reinforced. At one of the meetings, in Auckland, John Hart brought in several former All Blacks to remind us of who we were and what we were playing for. Being an All Black is a type of brotherhood, and an exclusive one at that. Most New Zealand males dream of being an All Black one day but a very small percentage of them achieve it. I'm told that since 1884, when the first New Zealand team was chosen, there have been less than a thousand. The heritage thing is important to the All Blacks but I suspect it takes on greater importance and significance when a player has finished playing. For the player still involved, he's playing for his team and his teammates and for his own satisfaction and enjoyment, even though he's conscious of the legacy of the jersey.

Reassembling for the first All Black test of the year is a bit like the first day of a new school year. It's a time to catch up with old friends, chat about what we've been doing since we last met, take the mickey a bit about games won and lost, meet the new boys and welcome them into the fold. At the back of the mind there's a little apprehension about what the year may bring. This particular year, there was also the buzz of everything being new and different.

Among the new boys was Christian Cullen, who had been outstanding in the Super 12. By June in other years, new players wouldn't have had the

opportunities to show how good they were, so Cullen had the Super 12 to thank for being an All Black so soon. There had been no doubt that he would be, with his rare talent, but without the Super 12 it may have taken several more months for him to be chosen. The Super 12, being so close to test level play, proved that he was ready. And how!

It didn't take him long. Three tries against Western Samoa, four in the next test, against Scotland. Seven tries in two tests. Not bad for a new guy. It was and remains a joy to play alongside him. His speed and ability to step off either foot are extraordinary and he brought a new dimension to the All Black game. With all due respect to Glen Osborne, "Cully" gave the outside backs added firepower and we felt in those early months that no one would be able to beat us.

Cullen is the most talented footballer I've played with. He's got ability that people haven't seen yet and I've seen him do things that no one else is capable of doing. His stint at centre in 1999 helped him read the game and should be of benefit to him back at fullback. I've no doubt that with Cullen around, my test try-scoring record will be short-lived.

What a combination in 1996 — the wise old heads of previous years plus new talent such as Christian Cullen, and the added bonus of having back from injury Andrew Mehrtens and Josh Kronfeld.

Little wonder that I almost felt sorry for Western Samoa after the first test. I say "almost". Scotland were dispatched at Carisbrook with as much emphasis, though I suspect we let them into the game in the second test, at Eden Park. Playing test rugby is as much a mental thing as it is physical and if before the game the focus gets fuzzy or during it the concentration slips, the performance suffers. We knew we could beat Scotland in Auckland and perhaps we subconsciously relaxed a little. Not much, but enough to give them more in the game than they should have had.

We were determined not to fall into the same trap in Wellington but because it was against Australia, we knew anyway that we had to be on our mettle. Australians, as familiar as we are with their style of play, are always difficult opponents because they're so competitive. Give them a centimetre and they'll take a kilometre. They are also, by and large, intelligent rugby players and I have to be careful how I express this in case I get misinterpreted and accused of saying that others are dumb. Rugby players in New Zealand reflect their society: they're a cross-section of everyone and of every type. It's an egalitarian game in New Zealand and always has been. That's not the case in Australia. Rugby there historically is based on the upmarket schools and universities. League is the game of the people. This is speaking generally of course. There are always exceptions. But because of the nature of the game in Australia, Wallabies from time to time can be more clinical about their game. They seem to be able to plot intricate moves on whiteboards, then

Christian Cullen, the most talented footballer I have played with, scores one of his three tries in his début test, against Western Samoa in Napier.

execute them on the field as if there was no opposition in the way. The Wallabies are also great innovators, as they have to be because they do not have the playing depth that we or South Africa have. The Brumbies for the last two or three years have been good examples of the Australian way of rugby, just as New South Wales Country used to be. Remember their "up-the-jumper" move?

This is a long-winded way of saying that All Blacks are always wary of Australia because as familiar as we are with what they do, there's always the chance of something different. In Wellington, therefore, there was no chance of us relaxing as we may have against Scotland in Auckland. We were focused. We were determined. And, as is often the case in Wellington, a southerly blew . . . and blew.

The 43-6 win at Athletic Park was later touted as being as close to the perfect game as it is possible to get. I know All Blacks from time to time strive for the perfect game, but it's not a realistic goal. Too many variables come into play in a test for anything approaching perfection. Tests for me come into the categories of bad (a loss), good, very good and fantastic. I suppose the Wellington defeat of Australia came into the fantastic category. We played the way we wanted to play, all of us were on top of our game, and we were in such form that the Wallabies saw very little of the ball. It was very satisfying because the result confirmed for us what we thought — that we had a team that could take on the world.

Until the next game. There is always a next game. Sit back on your laurels and think you're the bee's knees and you'll soon be on the losing side. It's one of rugby's great clichés that the next game is the important one. So it is. No one can afford to look too far ahead. Think of a rugby test series, or a Super 12 or an NPC, as a hurdles race. You're at the start line. Out ahead of you are 10 flights of hurdles. After the 10th flight is the finish line. Think what would happen if, when the gun goes, you lift your head to the finish line 110 metres in the distance and don't concentrate on the 10 hurdles in your way. Bang goes one hurdle. Crash goes another. Rattle goes another. Winners to the podium please, losers to the dressing room. Another day, another lesson.

Our next game was South Africa, a fortnight later in Christchurch. As it happened, it was the 300th test to be played by the All Blacks, an auspicious milestone that should have been marked by another majestic win. But no. It was marked by a win, but one that so easily could have been a loss. It was one of those days when things didn't go our way, when we were outmuscled in the forwards by the Springboks and out-thought — yes! — in the backs. There was a feeling that this test was a prelude of the tests to come in South Africa and if it was, then the Springboks gained the psychological advantage.

The long haul to South Africa had a stopover in Brisbane where we played the Wallabies again in the second match of the tri-nations. This was

Celebrating Frank Bunce's match-winning try in Brisbane with Andrew Mehrtens and Craig Dowd.

Frank Bunce feels the wrath of Michael Brial.

the game that was almost a repetition of the 1994 match in Sydney, the Wallabies scoring often and heavily in the first half and us clawing our way back into it in the second. On this occasion, however, we were able to win and took great satisfaction from the knowledge that although we were behind on the scoreboard, we didn't panic but just worked away on the way we wanted to play the game. We knew the points should come, and they did. Even so, it was a close-run thing, with Frank Bunce getting the winning try with just seconds left, having scooped it up when Christian Cullen had slipped over when it seemed he might score. It was justice that Bunce got the winning try because this had been the match in which he was the victim of an extraordinary flurry of punches from the Australian No 8, Michael Brial. Usually, when punches are thrown — and they're not all that frequent — it's a forward making a point or it's just a swing of an arm in the heat of an anguished moment. This attack, however, was extraordinary because it was apparently

ME OF RUGBY

ABSOLUTELY POSITIVELY
THE BEST IN MOVIES

384-44-44

The Dominion

premeditated, retaliation by Brial for some real or imagined transgression by Bunce in a match four years earlier! See what I mean about Australians being intelligent? New Zealanders wouldn't remember what had happened in games four months earlier, never mind four years.

In its own way, that test was important to us because it proved that we could retain our composure and stick to our game-plan even when we were down. It confirmed our confidence in ourselves that we were the better team over 80 minutes. We would need all that confidence, and all of the 80 minutes, in South Africa.

Just a word here on Frank Bunce. He was, to my mind, the most under-rated centre to play the game and was as talented as any I've played with in understanding the game and his role in it. He was the best player I knew for turning up at the right time to do the right thing. Playing outside him was easy and I learnt more from him than from any other player. And it was always good to be able to send players back into his zone so he could smash them!

Many New Zealanders have gone to South Africa on rugby trips, following the team around from match to match, and believe me, we've been grateful for the support. An oasis of black in a sea of green and gold. But I doubt that anyone who has been there really understands what it's like to play there unless they've been on the field. Matches there, and tests in particular, have a peculiar and distasteful atmosphere all of their own. The stadiums now are vast and, when the All Blacks are playing, are usually full and it's almost possible to feel the hate radiating down from the tiers of stands to focus on 15 guys in black. The South Africans en masse are not a nice people. They don't go to see a good game. A good game to them is one that is won by South Africa. They go to see their "Bokkies" and to see, more than anyone else, the All Blacks get thrashed. They don't care whether the rugby's good or not. In New Zealand, Australia and most other places, for all the partisan support that the home side enjoys, there is still an underlying appreciation of good play. At Twickenham, there's applause when the All Blacks score, even — still! — when there's a kick into touch (no one said they had to keep up with law changes).

But in South Africa there are no such niceties. It is not a pleasant place to be for a rugby player, for all the natural beauty of the land and the charm and friendliness of individuals. Speak to All Blacks who have toured there and, almost to a man, they'll say they hate the place, and this has nothing to do with whether they were there in the bad old days of apartheid or since.

Part of the enmity of course is because New Zealand and South Africa are the most competitive of rugby foes. The South Africans, and I don't want to start sounding like a bush psychologist here, are still an insular people and they are desperate to be recognised as being the best at whatever it is they do.

Previous pages: Marching girls and smoke provide a dramatic-looking entrance for the test against Australia at Athletic Park in 1996.

144

Some sort of inferiority complex lurks deep in the breast of every South African, especially every Afrikaner. They play rugby extremely well, and have done so for more than a century, but the one country that stands in their way of being recognised as the best is New Zealand. Therefore, we are the enemy, we are the black invaders.

It's not just in games that we get this feeling either. There is an air of contrivance off the field to beat us in any way they can. Don't think I'm being paranoid here. Earlier teams to South Africa will know the feeling well and I can entirely understand Laurie Mains, even if I don't agree with him, finding nefarious plotters at work upsetting our plans to win the World Cup in 1995.

The South African crowds also single out individual All Blacks who they think may be more influential than most on the outcome of a series. It used to be Sean Fitzpatrick and, if you listened to the crowd, he was evil personified, a walking Black Plague. When Fitzpatrick wasn't there to kick around any more, the crowds seemed to seize on me. I thrived on it. The more stick they gave me, the more extravagant would my gesture be when I scored. If I could dive and slide in front of a rowdier section of the crowd, then so much the better. The more they hated me, the more I enjoyed it. If they'd ignored me, I would have been disappointed.

In earlier days, All Black teams also had to contend with South African referees and I can only begin to imagine the frustration and anger our players must have felt. At least we don't have to contend with that now. It's hard enough as it is beating 15 obsessed over-sized hulks in green and gold without having also to find some way of beating the referee.

In 1996, we toured South Africa in the sense that we played midweek matches, but nothing of course like the 25 to 30 matches earlier teams had to endure. The tour is almost finished in the modern game and in most cases, particularly in South Africa, the general attitude is "Get in, get up and get out."

We were helped enormously in 1996 by John Hart being able to persuade the New Zealand Rugby Union board to take 36 players. By earlier standards, that was a huge number to take for eight matches. But Hart, meticulously organised as always, went to the board with an argument of irrefutable logic. We needed 21 players for the tests, he said, 15 players and six reserves, and to avoid some of them having to back up in midweek matches — and therefore having the potential to lessen our chances of winning the series — we needed another 15. The board, to its credit, saw the logic. It's not always that administrators have had the best interests of the players at heart. Some players would still be backing up, but not as many as before. And, in any case, we were still one big squad with every single one of us wanting a place in the test team. To consign a player to "the midweek

To the victors go the spoils: Cape Town in 1996 with the fruits of the first tri-nations series.

team" was not to say he wouldn't be playing in a test. They still had the chance to play their way in.

I sometimes wonder if the general public truly appreciates the attitude of players in an All Black squad, particularly an enlarged one of 36. All are All Blacks. There are no "superstars" or others — that's a public perception. We are the Three Musketeers times 12, all for one and one for all, united we stand etc etc. That's not just a theory or a principle, it's a fact. We are, in the best sense of the word, a team. When there is a tour such as South Africa in 1996, it's inevitable that some players are test players and some are not and that for practical, training purposes, there are two groups. The attitude of the test players is to play as well as they can so as not to let the rest of the team down. The attitude of the others is to play their games as well as they can, and therefore put pressure on for test places, and also so as not to let down the wider team. Before a test, the others support and help the test players in every way they can; similarly before midweek games, the test players do everything possible to smooth the way for those playing the next game.

That was the way it was in 1996. We knew we had a team capable of winning the series, and we also knew we had backup players equally capable

Gary Teichmann has me but I can still get the ball away as Walter Little looms.

if any of the test players were injured or lost form and were replaced. We were a strong touring party. Also a happy one.

We were a whole lot happier after the first test in Cape Town, and also a whole lot happier than we had been at halftime. As we'd predicted after the average match in Christchurch, the South Africans took us on with bulk and power — finesse is not one of the South African rugby player's strong suits. They were bigger than us, of that there was no doubt, and perhaps they were stronger too. But were they fitter, would they still be running around after 80 minutes like they were after 40? We thought not. The South Africans' defence was also very good. It was well organised and the players, as they had in Christchurch and in the tests in 1994, committed themselves to the tackle, knowing that in test matches, one single mistake can be the difference between winning and losing.

After half the game, they'd scored two tries and we'd scored two penalties. Within five minutes of the second half, we were 18-6 down. But, as in Brisbane, we didn't panic; we knew that we were still good enough to win providing we stuck to doing what we had planned to do. Our first try, by Glen Osborne benefiting from a break by Christian Cullen, ended an embarrassing try drought against South Africa. We hadn't scored a try against them since the second test in Wellington two years previously — 390 minutes of test rugby without a try.

As we'd thought they might, the Springbok forwards tired noticeably as the game wore on and our pack gradually gained dominance, providing the platform for yet another comeback win. In the end, we won by 11 points which we were told was a record margin for New Zealand in South Africa. Not bad for a team that had been 18-6 down.

The way the tour was structured, that was the last of the tri-nations matches so we were the first, and unbeaten, tri-nations champions. Now for the next phase. Three tests in consecutive weeks in a separate series.

Although All Blacks, like all other rugby players, stick to the tried and true one game at a time formula, we knew that winning the first test, in Durban, was absolutely critical. To lose the first test of a three-match series would make it just too difficult. Winning the first test would also mean the second in Pretoria could well decide the series. We wanted to kill it stone dead there, and not have to go to Johannesburg for the decider. The Pretoria crowd is bad enough. Johannesburg is infinitely worse and none of us who had been there the year before had any happy memories of the place. Far better to snatch the prize away from the South Africans before they could get a sniff of it at Ellis Park.

So we went to Durban with a hardened resolve, not just to win, but to win well. And, importantly, to start well. Though we'd won our last two tests by coming from behind, it's a risky practice. Far better to get the dominance early, get the points on the board and tell the South Africans, "Catch us if you can." The start at Kings Park was all we wanted. The forwards refused to buckle to the heavier Springboks and within four minutes we had the first try, with me benefiting from a strong run down the left touch by Glen Osborne and good follow-up work by the forwards when the move broke down. Christian Cullen also scored in the first half, also the beneficiary of the forwards' hard work, and by halftime we were 15-9 up. Of course that's not much of a lead, but it was a whole lot better than what we'd become used to in the previous two matches. Zinzan Brooke scored in the second half after I'd followed up a wipers kick by Walter Little that had the South African defence stretched too wide. They scored one try and although we were not completely dominant for the whole of the match, we felt we were always in control.

A word here for Simon Culhane, who was brought into the test team for Andrew Mehrtens, who had a knee injury. "Nibs", as he is popularly known (I suspect because his body shape was about as substantial as a pen nib), epitomised what I meant about all the members of the touring party being important and each individual contributing to the success of the whole.

Culhane was the ultimate team man and, though there wasn't much of him, we knew that he would never let us down. He'd shown it the year before at the World Cup and again in Italy and France, when he played each of the tests after Mehrtens was injured. Simon did everything expected of him in the Durban test, including kicking three valuable goals.

The tour was panning out the way we wanted it. We could win the series in Pretoria. If we played as we wanted to play, Johannesburg would be, in tennis terms, a "dead" match. Still a test match and still important because of that, but without the outcome of the series riding on it.

We had to put them away in Pretoria. We felt that if we didn't, the Springboks would then be on a high and Johannesburg would be the last place we'd want to meet them feeling like that.

You know the result. New Zealand 33, South Africa 26. Series win to New Zealand. The first series win in South Africa to New Zealand.

Simon Culhane ... doing everything expected of him.

Saying it quick like that makes it sound easy. It wasn't. They were every bit as hard and determined as we thought they'd be. They scored first, we got one back then I got another try, a kick and chase over André Joubert, to edge us into the lead. The lead extended. Then it closed. They tried everything they knew and a few things they made up on the spot. But nothing was going to get past the All Blacks with the mood we were in for the final few minutes. The forwards were magnificent, out on their feet but still finding reserves of energy from somewhere to hurl back the pretenders. There was guts and there was passion and there was pride. There was also the outrageous. With a lead of four points, Zinzan Brooke was hovering around first-five. Justin Marshall had the ball and Brooke screamed for it as only he could. Back it came. And whang! Another Brooke dropped goal, just to make it sure.

Culhane had left the field with an injured wrist and Jon Preston came on as first five-eighth, the first time he'd played in that position in a test since 1991. But as with Culhane, so with Preston. The value of the squad was there for all to see. He was no sooner on the field than he kicked one penalty, then added another from two metres inside the All Black half with six minutes left.

Much was made, and rightly so, of the All Blacks winning a series in South Africa for the first time, and how important that was to all the players who had been there before us and come away defeated and frustrated. John Hart before the match told us the whole world was watching because we could

make history at Loftus Versfeld that day. He also told us of some of the great players who, as great as they were, had tried and failed. We were playing for them, he said, just as we were also playing for the New Zealanders sitting hunched over television sets in the pre-dawn, and for the New Zealanders who had scrimped and saved to get to Pretoria for the match.

All this was true and we were conscious of both the heritage and of the support, and I remember seeing Murray Mexted and Don Clarke in Pretoria, and thinking that there were two great All Blacks who could not achieve what we could.

It was great that All Blacks of the past took satisfaction from our win, just as it's great that the nation rejoices when we do well, but the reality, the

The irrepressible Zinzan Brooke waits for a high five after his dropped goal in Pretoria.

Heading for a try in the 1996 decider in Pretoria.

bottom line, is that I'm not playing for anyone other than my teammates and myself. I play to do the best I can so as not to let the team or myself down. I'm sure that's the case for all of the All Blacks. Perhaps I'm still too young to appreciate the real values of heritage and nostalgia and maybe in later years I'll look back on Pretoria and think that it was historical justice that we dispensed on that day in August 1996.

All I know now is that I and my teammates did everything we could to win that match. After it, we were drained physically and emotionally. It was the peak of our endeavours.

We all had the motivation of winning a series in South Africa for the first time. Some of us had demons of 1995 that we wanted to exorcise. The feeling before the match was similar to what it had been before the Cape Town match against England in 1995. We were going to win. Whatever it took, whatever the punishment, we would win. It was an impenetrable resolve. It left us drained.

Hart talked to a few of us about making changes for the final test in Johannesburg to give us a break but decided he wouldn't make any because he didn't want to deny us the chance of a clean sweep. Having climbed our mountain, though, the Johannesburg test was a peak too far. We'd won the series. The motivation wasn't there, yet the Springboks still had the desire. They had to salvage something. And they did, but only the consolation prize.

10. Life without Fitzy

No matter what the reputation or history of a sporting team, there will always be good years and bad years. The better the team, the more the good years. But there will be bad years, even for the All Blacks. I shouldn't say "even" the All Blacks because they're a sporting team like any other. Players come and go, the opposition teams may be in the cycle of their good years, and it's unrealistic for the public to expect the All Blacks to win every match they play.

They don't and they never have, even if the rosy glow of nostalgia sometimes would have people think otherwise. As All Blacks, we'd love to win every game but we have to live in the real world and we know the facts of sporting life.

So when there are successful times, we know they're going to end some time. During 1996 and 1997, when the All Blacks were steamrolling all in their path and some by record scores, we didn't think that the end might come so soon.

I blame Sean Fitzpatrick. There's a bit of heresy for you. The decline in the All Blacks' fortunes began when the writing on the wall was plain to read: Fitzy's days were numbered. We knew it. He knew it. John Hart knew it.

There were other reasons of course why we didn't play as well as we would have liked in the British Isles at the end of 1997 and certainly didn't play as well as we should have in 1998. Fitzpatrick wasn't there any more.

It wasn't just Fitzpatrick either. The tour at the end of 1997 was the last for Zinzan Brooke and then we lost another key player, Frank Bunce, before the 1998 international season began. It was a triple whammy for the All Blacks. Three long-serving players, each inspirational in his own way, each fiercely proud of being an All Black, all gone.

Fitzpatrick, the most competitive player in the game, who, we felt, would sometimes stop at nothing to win, and who, we knew, opposition players were in awe of.

Brooke who would rise to the big occasion or, when he was needed the most, would deliver. He was always capable of doing something that would

Sean Fitzpatrick, one of the most competitive men to have played the game.

lift the whole team, such as his dropped goal against South Africa in Pretoria in 1996.

And Bunce, an All Black late in life who in his undemonstrative way would quietly go about his business, either defending heroically or attacking audaciously. American football has defensive and offensive lineups. Bunce would have slotted with equal facility into either.

All three were gone and their going made a difference. Players do come and go, that is true, and those who remain just have to get on with it and, in the history of the All Blacks, there seems to have always been someone to make the step up and carry on the torch for the next generation. But there are, and there have been at times in the past, players who are more difficult to replace than others. Losing Fitzpatrick, for example, I imagine would have been like the All Blacks in the early 70s when Colin Meads was no longer

there to lead on the field and to guide off it. It was similar when New Zealand cricket no longer had the services of Richard Hadlee. There would never be another Hadlee but there had to be someone to take his place. The interim process was the problem.

The loss of those three players should not be underestimated. Fitzpatrick had been an All Black since 1986. I was 12 when he first took the field for the All Blacks! The experience he brought to the team was invaluable and, until the knee injury that forced him out of the game troubled him, he was still playing as well as he ever had. Even when the knee injury pained him, he'd still play well, pushing aside such wimpish emotions as pain. There was nothing that he didn't know about rugby and no one would dare question him anyway.

Brooke, who had been an All Black for only a year less than Fitzpatrick

Ever-reliable Frank Bunce, this time in Pretoria outrunning Springbok centre Danie van Schalkwyk.

Always a man to rise to the occasion, Zinzan Brooke barrels Joel Stransky in Durban in 1996.

and Bunce, though he didn't get his chance until Laurie Mains took over as coach in 1992, had been playing for as long as Fitzpatrick. Such combined wisdom and experience cannot be replaced easily or overnight.

The loss of those three was, I think, the major contributing factor to our unhappy end in 1998. There were other reasons, as there will always be in sport, but not having them was the critical factor.

That was in the future though, as we began 1997 the way we'd finished off in 1996, feeling good as a team and knowing that we generally were better than any of the opposition. That came from self-belief, which every team has to have. If a team collectively doesn't have it, if it doesn't think it can win, rest assured it won't. It's what the Australian cricketers always have but when New Zealanders talk about them in this context, the word "cocky" is used rather than self-belief. I hope the All Blacks never get described as cocky, but I also hope that they always have the self-belief because if they don't, they'll be on a slippery downward slope. The self-belief is a collective thing within the team, but it also applies individually. I have to back myself in every game I play to step the opposition wing or to make the last-line defensive tackle or whatever it is, just as a prop has to back himself to be better technically and stronger than the prop he is marking, or an openside flanker to be quicker, more creative and anticipate better than the other No 7. If you don't think you can do it, you won't. That applies especially in test rugby where the line between victory and defeat is often a fine one and when matches are won not necessarily by the physically better team, but by the one that's mentally better.

The early matches in 1997 were, let's be brutally frank about it, a doddle. Fiji 71-5. Argentina 93-8 and 62-10. These were results that reflected the quality of the opposition and also the collective will of the All Blacks. We won each of those matches well because we were a better team and because we didn't let our standards slip, despite the inferior opposition. Sometimes against such teams it's possible to take it too casually, to let the concentration slip and not do yourself justice, even though you still might win by a reasonable margin.

The tri-nations matches weren't, to be honest, all that much more difficult. We felt we had the wood on them in each of the games and I think they sensed that too. The 55-35 win against South Africa at Eden Park was an extraordinary outcome against such a formidable and enduringly difficult opponent.

We came down to earth in the last match, against Australia at Carisbrook, which may have been the ultimate as a game of two halves. We scored 36 points in the first half and they scored none. If we'd continued, it would have been humiliating for them. But in the second half, they scored 24 and we scored none. It was a bizarre game. We were utterly dominant in the first half, they in the second. I know we didn't consciously relax in the second half; they just varied their tactics slightly, lifted their commitment and we very rarely had the ball to play with. We were fortunate we had such a buffer of points but then, had we not, the Aussies may not have fired as well in the second half as they did.

There were a few changes among the All Blacks for those domestic tests in 1997, some forced upon John Hart because of injury and some, I suspect, introduced as he looked forward either to the World Cup or to the inevitable day when some of the older guys would no longer be there. That was the year we were also without Jonah Lomu, who had that crippling kidney disease, and Tana Umaga played for the All Blacks for the first time. Significantly, we were also without Michael Jones for all but the first half of the first test, against Fiji. He was another player in the category of Fitzpatrick, Bunce and Brooke whose contributions, both on and off the field, would be sorely missed.

It's said that Jones wasn't as good a player after his knee injury in 1989.

Michael Jones is carried from the field during the test against Fiji in 1997.

If that's true, he must have been sensational in his first three years as an All Black. He was a devastating player in any game that I either played with or against him. He was — and remains — an extraordinary human being and the All Blacks could never have had a more exemplary role model.

The end of the golden weather started to settle in on the tour of the British Isles at the end of 1997. Being in Britain, I mean that literally. It really does get depressing there with grey skies seemingly all the time. Some people talk about the need for a global season for rugby and while I must say it's something I've never thought too much about, it would be good to be playing in Britain in June or July when at least there's a chance of some sun and warm weather. I'd been happy to miss the brief visit to England in November the previous year, when the All Blacks went in the guise of the Auckland Barbarians for two matches. I'd also missed Otago's tour there before the Super 12 and wasn't sad about that either.

The 1997 tour began in Wales and I can imagine how All Blacks of earlier years must have felt being there when Welsh rugby was strong and when they were the All Blacks' strongest opponents. The Welsh can be a charming people but they can also be obnoxious with their constant references to their past glories and their hopes for future ones. We played Llanelli at Stradey Park and, I suppose inevitably, we were reminded all the time about that dark and distant day when Llanelli beat the All Blacks 9-3. It's a quaint little ground and it was packed with passionate Welsh, but there was no chance of them beating us this day. We won 81-3 which if nothing else should have reinforced to them the fact that there is now a vast gulf between club and international play.

Significantly, we were captained against Llanelli for the first time by Justin Marshall. Sean Fitzpatrick was struggling because of his knee injury and there were doubts that he would play at all on the tour. If it was anyone else, they would have been at home with their leg up, contemplating the rest of their life. But Fitzpatrick's iron will was never something to underestimate and we knew that if he could take the field on one leg, he would.

It was never stated by John Hart, but there was a general feeling within the All Blacks that Marshall as captain was a stopgap measure, a sort of caretaker captain between what we could now see as the end of the Fitzpatrick era and the start of the Taine Randell era. It was always apparent that Randell would be the captain one day but first he had to secure a position in the test team. The captaincy wasn't an issue then. It was just something that everyone accepted was the position. That would change.

I had no problem with Marshall as captain. There's no doubting his ability or his desire when he plays for the All Blacks and, at the time, he was playing some great rugby. Hart and the other selectors wanted someone to lead the team who was sure of his place and Justin fitted that requirement, and they also wanted someone with the passion to fire up the troops when necessary. As a halfback, Marshall could talk with the best of them.

With hindsight, making Marshall the captain on that tour was a mistake. Not through any fault of his, though he may have been less diplomatic than he should have been with referees at times, but quite simply because he had no captaincy experience. He joked about his only previous experience being captaining the Mataura under 7s.

The non-playing captain, Sean Fitzpatrick, and his interim replacement, Justin Marshall.

I think it was a mistake to thrust the test captaincy onto someone who had had no experience, especially when there were other options, interim or otherwise. Zinzan Brooke, though he treated the tour as something of a farewell tour for himself, would have been a stronger, more understanding leader and Randell, who was on the side of the scrum, could also have been given the job, especially as he had Fitzpatrick off the field for any guidance. Todd Blackadder led the midweek team on that tour but could not have been considered because there was no place in the test team for him.

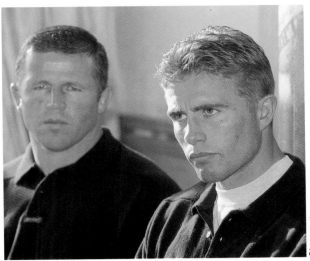

Photosport

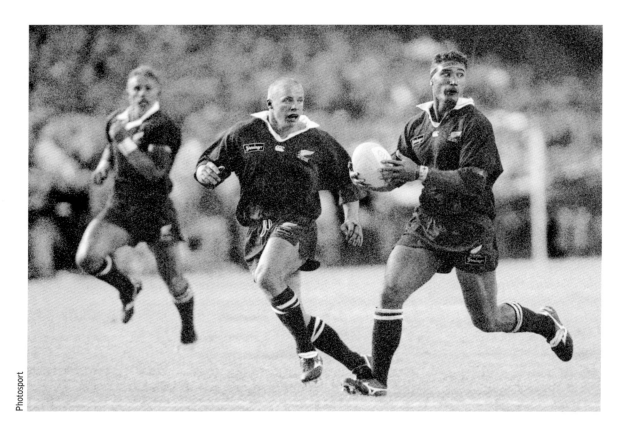

Andrew Blowers, with Christian Cullen and Justin Marshall, attacks against Ireland in 1997 – the match in which he was chosen ahead of Josh Kronfeld.

There were problems in other areas too, especially with Josh Kronfeld. He seemed to have lost confidence and it was no real surprise when Andrew Blowers was picked in his place for the test against Ireland. It was the first time he had missed a test for which he was available since the Sydney test in 1995, when the circumstances surrounding his dropping were mysterious indeed.

There was no mystery about why he wasn't picked for the Irish test. Hart felt that Blowers was playing better than him and there also seemed, watching from the sidelines, to be a difference of philosophy between Josh and John Hart. This happens on rugby tours from time to time because anyone who reaches the top in sport has to be strong-willed and it's inevitable that sometimes there will be personality clashes. In the wider interests of the team as a whole, such differences are usually privately aired and sorted out.

I think Hart also felt the need to play Blowers on the open side because the attrition rate for that position is such that it could be foolhardy to rely on just one player, no matter if that one was Kronfeld who, at his best, is far and away the best in the world. Blowers was playing fine rugby at the time and Hart I think was justified in putting him in the No 7 as insurance against the day when Kronfeld might not be available. And as someone who's been close to Josh for quite a few years, I know the punishment his body takes during a game. He can slump down in the dressing room after games and, to look at him, you'd swear he'd played his last game and was fit only for a medical school lecture on how much the human body can withstand. But give him a couple of days and he's bounding around the park again, putting his body through even more.

So Hart was justified, but of course Kronfeld didn't see it that way and, in his inimitable fashion, he complained publicly that Blowers would be wearing "my jersey". Josh got on the field at Lansdowne Road as a replacement anyway and his disagreement with Hart may have been just the boost he needed, a little replenishment of the motivation juices.

I was a distant observer of all of this. Hart never consulted me and there was no reason to expect him to. I was by then a fairly senior All Black but nowhere near as senior as the inner sanctum of people such as Fitzpatrick, Zinzan Brooke and Bunce, and it was to them that Hart turned if he was in need of advice or just wanted to talk things over.

As we had in South Africa the year before, we had 36 players so there were two effective teams and there was no need therefore for test players to back up in midweek matches. It made the tour more enjoyable because there was less pressure. We knew precisely what we had to focus on and that's what we did. Aside from the Llanelli game, it was a test each week and that was that. It was the end of the year, though, and it had been a long year and we were just waiting for it to be over. We'd been playing since late February, training since January, and it was now November and I can't think of any other physical contact sport that has such a long season and asks so much of its top players. American footballers and basketballers, who have compact, high-pressure seasons, would tell us we were mad if they ever knew what was asked of us. Tennis players, golfers and Formula One drivers all have long seasons with maybe only a month or two break; but while it's pointless comparing the sports, none of them undergoes the physical confrontation that rugby players do match in and match out. When professional rugby first began, I thought the fact players were being paid would enable them to stay in the game longer because there was less need for them to develop tandem careers, the other to serve them after rugby. Now I'm not so sure. The constant diet of rugby at a high level is extremely demanding, both physically and mentally, and unless there are some changes to scheduling, I fear players will have a shorter active career rather than longer. There is an element of Catch 22 of course. The administrators need the extra tests and extra competitions to earn the money to pay the players. There has to be a balance, but it certainly hasn't been found yet.

One of the saving graces of the 1997 tour was that we played in stadiums

such as Old Trafford and Wembley. While I'm not a traditionalist and a rugby ground to me is a rectangle of grass marked out with white lines and goalposts at either end, it was good to be able to play at such grounds. Variety is always good on tour, especially in Britain. It was good too that the grounds were soccer grounds and we could revel in the history and tradition of them without being bombarded about great rugby matches that occurred on them (and in England, great rugby matches mean defeats of the All Blacks). It was refreshing to wander around a ground such as Old Trafford and reflect on the might of Manchester United over the years, or to wander around Wembley and visualise the hordes of soccer supporters there for the FA Cup final or for internationals.

What wasn't refreshing was the actions of the England team after we beat them — beat them! — at Old Trafford. The score, if anyone needs reminding, was 25-8. New Zealand 25, England 8. Yet they pranced around as if they'd won the match, going from one side of the ground to the other, waving and clapping. If they'd had a cup, they would have waved it aloft. I know they were just thanking their supporters, but it came across as arrogant, which is how I find the English rugby players. They're not a pleasant team to play and they're no good to meet individually afterwards — two reasons why All Blacks hate losing to them. Speaking to players from other countries, I know they too reserve a special love for beating the English. They're just so patronising it makes me want to be sick. They claim to have invented the game and think they still run it. They can't even play it properly. They're a negative, spoiling team. The offside law is there to be broken, they constantly infringe in rucks and mauls, they kill the ball every chance they get. The England team, and the lesser English teams we play from time to time, seem more concerned about stopping the opposition from scoring rather than trying to score themselves. It is a negative, frustrating way to play the game and if all rugby was like that, I would have stopped playing years ago.

It didn't help our mood of course that we could only draw the second test against England at Twickenham. A draw to the All Blacks is as good as a loss. Perhaps worse, because a draw doesn't carry with it the same urgency to improve next time. A draw against England is terrible because it goes without saying that the English will treat it as a win and it will be hailed as one of the great days of English rugby. We were glad to get out of London at the end of that tour and, sitting and thinking on the flight home, I knew that we hadn't played as well as we should have and that we had let ourselves down. I didn't for a second imagine that what was to come could be worse.

The next year began as the previous one ended, against England. But for various reasons, it was a poor England team. Some of the better England players couldn't get releases from their clubs, which just showed how idiotic and short-sighted England was when professionalism began, and others were

Scoring in Dublin, despite the attentions of Eric Ellwood.

injured. The tour should never have gone ahead or, if it did have to, since it was England B they should have played New Zealand B.

The All Blacks should not have played that England team. It was demeaning test rugby. The signs were there from the start when Australia beat them 76-0. That put us on a hiding to nothing. If we couldn't beat them by a similar score, we would be seen as failures. We knew, going into the matches in Dunedin and Auckland on successive Saturdays, that all they would be trying to do would be to minimise the scores against them and that if we didn't beat them comprehensively, we'd be criticised. The two tests were meaningless mismatches and didn't feel like proper tests. I didn't take much satisfaction from either one of them and the sooner they're forgotten, the better.

It was a difficult time for the All Blacks. We knew we'd be without Zinzan Brooke, we guessed we'd be without Sean Fitzpatrick and then we found we were without Frank Bunce as well. He'd gone off to France to arrange a playing contract and somehow missed being home in time and was told by John Hart he wasn't wanted. I don't know all the precise circumstances, but I do know it was a sad way for Frank to end his All Black career. He deserved to be treated better than some joke of a player who missed a flight.

Taine Randell, to no one's surprise, was made captain and it was a decision with which I agreed at the time. I never dreamt, though, that the season would turn out the way that it did and that he would be under such immense pressure, far too much pressure for any one person to bear. I don't think that sort of pressure should be placed on anyone. The more losses as the tri-nations developed, the more it seemed that Randell and Hart moved further apart. There was no doubt that the losses in 1998 led to splits within the All Black camp and that some players were decidedly unhappy. Sharp words were spoken when there was a need for quiet reason; the team needed to draw closer together but instead the splits widened. Some players were openly critical of Randell, some of Hart. I don't blame Taine and neither do I blame John Hart.

I do think now that perhaps Taine had been made captain too early and that someone, perhaps Robin Brooke, should have been the captain as an interim measure on much the same basis as Justin Marshall had been appointed the year before. Taine needed more time to grow into the job and also to make his place in the test team more secure, though no one ever could doubt his ability or his commitment.

The unique thing about Taine is that he is extremely intelligent and perhaps was on too different a level for some of the All Blacks. He had long been earmarked as the captain of Otago and in a system such as Otago's, that was relatively easy. There's an ingrained ethos and system in Otago that everyone understands and accepts. It's not imposed by the captain or the

Edging ahead of Austin Healey for a try against England in Auckland.

165

coach. It's been there for years and carried on by succeeding generations of players and reinforced by each crop of senior players. When Taine took over as captain of Otago, there were players behind him such as John Leslie and Brendon Timmins who had been with Otago since the early 90s, and there was the next level down such as myself and Anton Oliver who were also imbued with the Otago way of doing things. It allowed Taine to ease into the captaincy without any problems.

With the All Blacks, it wasn't so easy. It's a totally different environment because there are players from different provinces who come with their own way of doing things. There's the Auckland ethos and the Canterbury ethos and all of this has to be melded together for the overall good of the All Blacks. I think that Taine in 1998 found it difficult to do this at the same time as he was trying to establish himself as a worthy test player. It was different for Fitzpatrick in 1992 when he took over as captain because he had already been a part of the All Blacks then for six years. Taine, though he'd been an All Black first in 1995, had a much harder and more demanding introduction.

The fact we were without experienced old hands such as Fitzpatrick, Brooke and Bunce and, midway through, Michael Jones as well, just compounded it all. The guys who should have been supporting Taine, who should have been the lieutenants to his captain, were not there any more.

The lonely burden of the captaincy ... Taine Randell leaves the Sydney Football Stadium after loss No 5.

Christian Cullen there in support, as always, against Australia in Sydney in 1998.

167

For all his keen intelligence, Taine was not all that articulate in 1998 — he seemed to have difficulty in getting across what he wanted to say. It may have been a lack of confidence in his role, it may have been because he knew that there were some players who felt he shouldn't be captain, and it may also have been because he is, like me in many ways, a private individual. I like my space and I'm quite happy being on my own at times, and I'm sure Taine is like that too. But he couldn't be on his own.

We also had a lot of new players in 1998; for a while they seemed to be coming and going, and they needed leadership that Taine was unable to provide. It was then that we needed someone else to stand up and take the lead, but no one did. I don't mean usurp Taine's role. I mean someone should have done what Zinzan Brooke often did in the past, taking on a surrogate leadership role, either on the field or off it. All teams have these guys who can inspire the rest of the team, but in 1998 we didn't.

Through all this, we never stopped trying. All Blacks are very proud people and we did everything we could to try to win. But there are times when you've just got to accept that the opposition are better than you and that was sometimes the case in 1998, especially Australia in Christchurch when they just hammered us.

But there were times also when we were dreadfully unlucky. We should have beaten South Africa in Durban and we so nearly did. James Dalton saying afterward that he had not forced the ball for the match-winning try was no consolation at all. It shouldn't have got to that. We should have put them away before that.

And there were other times, such as the Australian match in Sydney, when individual brilliance made the difference. On this occasion it was Matt Burke, who is one of the finest to ever play for Australia. There were mistakes by All Blacks at crucial times, some refereeing decisions which we could have questioned if we'd felt there was any point in it, some other factors that were small in isolation but loomed large when taken collectively.

All these circumstances contrived to give us a bad year. But the ironic thing about it was that I felt we weren't far away. We still had the talent, we still had the will. We were not a bad team. I wouldn't go so far as to say we were an unlucky team. We were a team with problems, of that there was no doubt, but the problems were not insurmountable and I felt that once we got on top of them, we would be a team capable of winning the World Cup.

11. End of a dream

The motto of the Special Air Service is "Who Dares Wins". That's fine by me, that's a concept to which any sportsman can relate; in fact, should relate. But as far as the military and I are concerned, that's about as far as it goes. I had never dreamt when I was a boy of being a soldier, I had never wanted to be a soldier. Yet there I was early in 1999, playing soldiers as part of the early buildup to World Cup year, to the All Blacks trying to regain the most prized trophy in world rugby.

What the news media called a boot camp — and it wasn't that at all, that's an Americanism anyway — had been devised by John Hart as a means of testing our physical and mental toughness, of pushing us toward limits of physical endurance and mental pressure that we'd never be subject to on a rugby field.

The SAS are the hard nuts of the New Zealand defence force. They're the élite, they're the best of the best from all the other regiments and units. Much of what they actually do in the defence of New Zealand is top secret, and I didn't want to know anyway.

What we did during the few days with them is secret as well. I can talk generally about what was involved but the details remain between me, the other All Blacks and the soldiers who were our instructors. What we did was extremely difficult and demanding and part of the point of it was that we All Blacks shared the common difficulties, even danger, and for the details to be made public would somehow detract from the special bond we all felt afterwards.

It was devised as a test of our character and, to a certain extent, our fitness, and it was certainly that. Its point was to give Hart and others of the All Black management team a better insight into the makeup of the players they were entrusting with the job of winning the cup.

I can say that we didn't indulge in the fantasy image of the SAS troopers living off the land for nights on end or of jumping out of aeroplanes or of crawling on our bellies for hours behind "enemy" lines. Neither did we get crash courses in any of the array of weapons the SAS has at its disposal.

Photosport

These were the pleasant
parts the public was
allowed to see ... rugby
training army-style with
the Special Air Service
in 1999.

Photosport

We didn't do anything that is part of the daily or weekly routine of the SAS troopers. Everything we did was devised by the regiment, in conjunction with the All Black management, specifically for us. The whole camp was about mental toughness, putting us in positions we'd never been before and testing us to go beyond our previous mental limits.

We knew after it all, and this was part of the plan of course, that no matter what challenges we faced later, nothing would be worse or more demanding than what we had gone through. The exercises we were put through were mentally and physically demanding and the object of it all was to complete it, to fulfil the SAS credo: Do whatever it takes to get it done.

For the most part, we were in groups of four in an exercise that lasted about a day and a half. With me were Robin Brooke, Mark Hammett and Bruce Reihana, and I found out more about those three guys in that day and a half than I could ever have done no matter how many games I'd played with or against them, no matter how many tours we may have done together. Each of them found out a hell of a lot more about me.

We had an SAS trooper with us all the time, though he was there for more of a watching brief than any intention of helping us. He knew what we were going through but if there was an easier way to do something, he wouldn't tell us. We knew we couldn't give up. No matter how tired, no matter how hungry or thirsty, no matter how difficult the task, we just could not give up. Sometimes we went close to giving up, but that would have been unforgivable. An extraordinary feeling of camaraderie developed between the four of us. Together, we worked just so hard to get through it. We all helped each other get through the bad times. I was lucky with the army boots I wore but Mark Hammett had terrible problems with blisters and we all felt for him. He, despite the pain he must have been in, gritted his way through it.

I was closer to breaking point during that day and a half than I've ever been but I'm pleased I went through it. It gave the four of us something special that is between just us.

We felt like dicks at the end though. We had to cook for ourselves with the equipment issued to us but we could find nothing to drink out of so we made do with the empty cans that had had food in them. It was only when it was all over that we learned the holder for our water bottles, which had been attached to our belts, was really a cup. Think beyond the square. That was another lesson.

I don't know if any of the All Blacks really enjoyed it all. Maybe Josh Kronfeld, he likes that sort of stuff. Enjoyment was not the word, more satisfaction that we completed it, that we were put to some pretty severe tests but that we came through.

A few months later, when we were in camp in Palmerston North just before we left for the World Cup, we were all put on a bus and told we were going to Taupo for some promotion. We never made it to Taupo. We got as far as the Desert Road and the bus ploughed off into the stark landscape that is the army training ground north of Waiouru. There was a car parked by the side of the road and out jumped one of the SAS troopers we'd met earlier. Follow me, he said. Some of the boys started laughing, guessing what was in store. Others groaned, "Oh no, here we go again", and others were just deflated. I think I was one of the groaners.

This time, though, it wasn't a day and half. Just eight or nine hours. "Just" eight or nine hours. On with the overalls, the boots, the blindfolds. It was amazing, now we knew what to expect, how we all got stuck in and just got on with it. It was three separate exercises on that occasion and the SAS guys remarked how much better we were.

The SAS was commanded at the time by the new All Black manager, Andrew Martin, though the link between our playing soldiers in 1999 and his appointment nearly a year later was entirely coincidental. It goes without saying, though, that he would have known a few things about us that no previous All Black manager ever could have known.

The SAS reported to John Hart and Mike Banks on the results of the exercises, evaluating us individually in terms of physical and mental stamina and in leadership qualities. How those results were used, I've got no idea. And maybe I don't want to know.

I'm a rugby player and I should be judged by what I do on the field. I'm not even fussed about fitness testing that is so much a part of rugby these days. It's the fashionable thing to do, measuring players for this and that, but what they don't do is measure the size of a player's heart or his passion. I know there's a place for scientific fitness testing and other evaluations such as the SAS gave us, but I don't set any great store by them. Partly that's the rebel in me, bucking the system just for the sake of it. The All Blacks' fitness advisor during the Hart years, Martin Toomey, knew very well that I had no regard for all the tests he put me through. It's only in the last two or three years that I have seen some merit in the fitness testing because I've been able to judge where I'm at. There are absurd sides to fitness testing, though. Look at the fuss made about Jonah Lomu when he ran a very slow three kilometres during a fitness test once. What did that prove? That he wasn't quick over three kilometres. So what? It's what he does on the rugby field that counts.

Would I go through the SAS's peculiar form of torture again? If it was a prerequisite for getting in the All Blacks, maybe. If it was simply a matter of choice, a resounding no. Never. No way. I think everyone found it difficult. I suspect only Josh would volunteer to do it again.

The two episodes with the SAS reinforced to us that the management would leave nothing to chance in its planning for the World Cup. And that was fine by me. Everything we did in 1999 was geared toward the cup; it was the single focus throughout the year, even though we had the Super 12 and the tri-nations along the way. The cup was the siren song in the distance and nothing, we felt, could get in our way.

I knew that when the Super 12 was finished, the All Blacks would have my sole concentration. The two overlapped in the last fortnight of the Super 12. The Highlanders were in Wellington for the last round-robin match against the Hurricanes when the first All Black crisis of the year occurred. John Hart wanted to name his first team of the year, to play New Zealand A in Christchurch, in the week before the Super 12 final. He therefore needed to name a captain as well. There had been public and media speculation for some time about whether Taine Randell would keep the job or whether it would go to someone else. My name had been bandied about and I admit that I had discussed the captaincy with Hart. My view, as I told John, was that I would only do it if there was no one else. I didn't think it would have been appropriate for me to be captain for several reasons, one that being at fullback or on the wing are not the most ideal positions from which to captain a team and another that I didn't think I'd be able to get through to the whole team.

I also wasn't as secure as I had been in the past. The death of my father late the previous year had hit me hard and, without him to turn to, I really didn't have anyone to go to for advice or just to listen to me. I didn't think I was in the best frame of mind to captain the All Blacks. My captaincy experience wasn't extensive anyway. I'd led the New Zealand Academy against Ireland A in 1997 and the Highlanders for three games in 1998 when Taine was injured, but otherwise that was pretty much it.

I told Hart that Anton Oliver should do the job and he, Hart, said he had been thinking of Robin Brooke. But Brooke felt his game was improving after a bit of a lull and he'd rather be left to concentrate on his own game rather than have the burden of captaincy as well.

In Wellington, Hart spoke to Oliver but Anton said he'd spoken to his father about it and didn't feel he was ready for such a responsibility. He said he'd rather consolidate his place in the team and perhaps look at the captaincy some time in the future.

It left Hart without any options but to stay with Taine Randell and he told him that. Taine admitted to me that they were confusing times for him because he thought he would not be captain and he had said in an interview, with *NZ Rugby Monthly*, that this was the case. The announcement preceded the magazine's publication and it had to hurriedly, and no doubt at considerable expense, cut the pages of Taine's interview before distribution.

It was overall a clumsy and not particularly enjoyable way to arrive at deciding on an All Black captain, especially as three of the supposed contenders, Taine, Anton and myself, were all Highlanders teammates and heading immediately from Wellington to Cape Town where we had to play the Stormers in the Super 12 semifinal.

It was after we'd won that match that Hart phoned each of the Highlanders, still in Cape Town, and told us of our selection; the team was publicly announced while we were on our way home.

It would have been better, I think, to have delayed the naming of the team until after the Super 12 final at Carisbrook on the following Sunday against the Crusaders. The last thing the Highlanders needed, especially the ones who were new All Blacks, in the week of the Super 12 final was to be questioned about the All Blacks. I felt that the New Zealand union erred in allowing Hart to name the team at such an inappropriate time, though he argued logically that there was not enough time to delay it. One of the reasons was that there were players in both teams, the All Blacks and New Zealand A, no longer involved in the Super 12.

Though I'd suggested Anton to John, I had no real problem with Taine. He had been through a lot the previous year, shouldering more pressure than any one person should bear, but he had improved as a captain. He was handling things better; the experience of winning the NPC with Otago in 1998 and then the Highlanders getting into the final of the Super 12 had been the tonic he needed. The weight of despair that comes from losing had been lifted from him.

Taine and I were actually opposing captains later in the year when the All Black World Cup squad, in camp in Palmerston North, had the "secret" game, which was our only match between the tri-nations and the opening game of the World Cup. Only a few guys who had been injured and needed game time, or who had not played much of the tri-nations, were allowed to play for their provinces in the NPC. For the rest of us, the squad game was our only game before the cup. It was a bizarre match, not because it was All Blacks against All Blacks with a few Manawatu players filling in gaps, but because it was in front of only a few spectators: the All Black management, a few other people who had been carefully screened and a group of Massey students who just happened along; maybe a total of 30 spectators. In terms of crowd noise and reaction, it was like playing a Shell Trophy match in front of empty stands. There was no atmosphere, no "bite". No cheers, no boos in a game that meant nothing. It was a full-on match, though, because guys were playing for test places. The referee was Colin Hawke who, like us, was sworn to secrecy. It must have been the least-publicised match All Blacks have ever played.

But it was as tough a game as I've been in. I captained the "B" team against the supposed test lineup that was led by Taine and we were thrashed. It was a very frustrating game because we'd been set up to lose and I thought

it would have served a more useful purpose if the teams had been evenly matched. But John Hart had devised it with specific thoughts in mind: he wanted to see various combinations and how some players reacted, so that was the way it was. It wasn't a game I enjoyed though. I play to win, not to make up the numbers.

If I could have, I would have much preferred to play a few games for Otago in the NPC but it was strictly laid down who could and who couldn't. As a principle, I believe the best players should continue to play in the NPC because that is our prime domestic competition. There should be some flexibility, though, and if All Blacks want to miss a game or two to give themselves more recovery time, they should be able to. In the end, common sense prevails. I certainly wouldn't like to see the day when no All Blacks play in the NPC at all. That idea was floated for a while and as far as I can see, it is an idea without merit.

The early matches in 1999 followed a similar pattern to previous years: no real challenges. The New Zealand A match was in effect a trial, though everyone involved was at pains to say that it wasn't, and the test at Albany against Samoa was, I'm sad to say, another mismatch. New Zealand rugby

Still smiling at this stage ... John Hart and me before the South African test in Dunedin in 1999.

Justin Marshall and me, in a souvenired French jersey, relax after the win in Wellington. Careful readers will note that it's a Nike jersey.

needs to do everything it can to develop Samoan rugby but I don't think it helps their cause by playing the All Blacks if they're going to be beaten by big scores all the time. At least the game allowed me to continue my love affair with Albany. I scored four tries to go with the five I'd scored there against Fiji and the five I scored for the Academy against Ireland A.

Even France, the first real test of the year, wasn't a test at all. It was a joke. Whatever France were doing, they weren't all that serious about beating New Zealand in a test. They had players missing or being played out of position and it seemed to us like one big experiment on their part. That's fine for them because I suppose it proved ultimately to be of some benefit to them, but tests to us are sacred and should not be devalued for other purposes.

Of course they didn't do the All Blacks any favours either. We had to beat them and beat them well otherwise we would have been publicly caned, every so-called expert in the land reaching for a phone to call talkback radio and give everyone else the benefit of their views.

The only memorable thing about the French test was that it was the last at Athletic Park. It was a day for nostalgia for older people and looking back at some of the great matches that had been played there, but for me it was just time to move on. I'd had some good games there, especially for Otago,

Photosport

**A new brand.
Jonah Lomu and
me decked out in the
new All Black gear.**

but really it was a rundown ground and it was time for it to be pensioned off. Wellington people deserve their new stadium and the way they — and the Hurricanes — responded showed no one was missing Athletic Park at all. I know I don't.

As the tri-nations developed we felt we were playing well enough, even though we didn't score as many tries as we would have liked, especially in the win against Australia in Auckland. I think in the back of our minds all the time was the World Cup and though the tri-nations tests were important, as all tests are, they were just the overture to the main event. Even the loss to the Wallabies in Sydney didn't upset us all that much because, if nothing else, it quelled any latent complacency. We know the Australians' play as well as our own but on that night, fired up as they were in their new Olympic stadium, they were too good for us. We didn't like the loss, but it gave us areas of our game to focus on for the cup. Had we won in Sydney, we may not have gone to Britain with the same resolve. We may have felt that we were good enough.

We felt that we were the best team in the competition. That's not bragging or over-confidence, that was a frank appraisal of our opponents before the competition began. We knew that we could win each game providing we did what we intended to do and played as well as we knew we could. We had the players to do the job.

For all that, we were apprehensive in the leadup to the cup because it is such a big, significant event and as much as players may try not to, they get sucked in by the hype as well as everyone else. Painting murals of All Blacks on Air New Zealand aircraft didn't help us much. All Blacks like to fly in quietly and do the business, not make some grand triumphal entry as if they

Does Taine Randell look faintly embarrassed as he stands in front of the mural with which an Air New Zealand aircraft was plastered? He probably was.

Photosport

only have to show up to win. That was where the lines got a bit blurred. All of New Zealand, it seemed, had this notion that we could not be beaten, a notion that may have been aided by all the advertising and promotions and also the downright stupid talk about victory parades before we'd even played a match. That is not the All Black way and it was not our way. We were as well prepared as we could be and we were quietly confident that we could win providing things went well for us. That is not the same thing as arrogantly strutting around as if we had the cup already won. We don't do that.

One overriding problem with the World Cup was that we were built up so much as the probable winners, built up by forces beyond our control, that when we didn't, the disappointment, deflation and, we discovered, the anger was so much more keenly expressed and felt.

It was in an uncertain future when we arrived in Britain for the fourth World Cup. Our biggest concern, or at least the biggest concern that involved me, was in team selection. John Hart had a problem and was faced with the difficult decision of which outside backs to choose and where to put them. The problem was that if he had me at fullback, a placement with which I was entirely happy, he had three guys who deserved to get in to fit into two positions — Jonah Lomu, Tana Umaga and Christian Cullen. Not only that, he had four guys if you include me who were similar players in that their strengths were in having the ball tucked under an arm and going for it. He

Tana Umaga seems to be getting away from me at training. The year of the World Cup was a breakthrough year for him.

179

hadn't played Lomu other than as a substitute in the tri-nations yet he knew the psychological value of Lomu at the World Cup, especially against England. Cullen was too powerful and talented a runner to be left out, 1999 was Umaga's breakthrough year, Lomu could be a devastating player and Alama Ieremia couldn't be left out because he was the midfield strongman who created the space or the time for those outside him.

I discussed this with John Hart and expressed my views quite strongly but he disagreed. I'm not going to criticise him for what he decided because he made that decision in what he thought was in the best interests of the team and of the individuals. We disagreed, that's all, and the last thing I want to do is join the Hart-bashing that horrified and disgusted me after the cup. No man, least of all one who was trying to do his best for his country, deserved the sort of public condemnation he suffered, especially condemnation by people who were largely uninformed or misinformed or who were just looking for someone to blame for the disappointment they felt.

The downfall of the team, though, may have been in the selections that were made. By having me at fullback, Umaga and Lomu on the wings and Cullen at centre, with Ieremia going to second five-eighth, I felt the team as a whole was relying too much on individuals, no matter how brilliant. The effect was that we became an uncreative team. It was hard at times for me to become involved. That's not me speaking from a selfish point of view, but because the others were doing what they did best and that's what they were chosen to do. In other words, I felt that we weren't making the best use of the resources we had.

I voiced these concerns to John before we'd played our first game and my fears were realised as the cup progressed. It gave me no satisfaction to see that this was so.

Such concerns weren't readily apparent in the opening game against Tonga because that game went pretty much as we thought it would. We knew they'd throw everything at us but that gradually we would wear them down. That was the way it panned out and there was no real concern in the All Black camp after the game.

Even against England, the game we had to win to secure the better side of the draw, the problems of us being an uncreative team did not really surface because it was our defence that was most critical in winning that game, not our attack. England had so much of the possession that they should have won the game twice over, and would have against any lesser team. I was proud of the way the All Blacks defended in that game and of the way we were able to take the few scoring opportunities available to us.

I think too that the England game created in the minds of the New Zealand public the view that once we'd won it, nothing else really mattered. It had been built up to such an extent that it was seen as a quasi-final even

Christian Cullen attacks from centre against Tonga in the World Cup, but was this the best use of his immense talents?

Overleaf: Scoring at Twickenham in the crucial World Cup pool match against England.

though it was only our second pool match. It was as if once having won at Twickenham and secured the "soft" side of the draw, the cup was already ours. We were only too well aware that was not the case, but public opinion is a powerful force.

The third pool match, against Italy, served to deceive. The Italians were not at all a strong side and we did more or less what we wanted and relying on individual brilliance rather than teamwork was never going to be exposed against such a side. It was gratifying that I scored three times in that match to become the New Zealand record holder for test tries, and satisfying too that my mother was there to see it, but it otherwise wasn't hugely significant to me. Such records come if someone plays long enough and I'd rather score a try to win a test than score just to add to a personal tally. Rugby is the ultimate of team games and it's for the team that an individual should play, not for personal rewards or glory.

Scoring against Italy at Huddersfield ... the match in which I broke John Kirwan's test tries record.

We were more exposed against Scotland in the quarterfinal, especially in the second half when we were without Andrew Mehrtens and had lost some of our direction and control. This is no criticism of Tony Brown, who replaced Mehrtens, but the signs were beginning to show.

And so to France, the game that destroyed the hearts of a nation, so we learned, and certainly destroyed the hopes of the All Blacks. I thought then, and still do now, that we were a better team than the French. We had better individuals and we were better as a team. But we lost. Mehrtens said we were "outpassioned". Maybe we were because the French certainly took a lot of passion into the game, something they can do every so often but certainly not in every game they play. They run hot and cold as a national team and on this occasion they were far too hot for us. Better team we may have been, but they were better than us on the day. That's the way it is in sport sometimes and that's what followers have to accept, as unpalatable as it may be.

I don't think, with all the benefit of objective hindsight, that we could have prepared any better than we did for the semifinal. We'd been criticised for being pampered pets by going off to the south of France before the quarterfinal but that criticism, like much levelled at the All Blacks, was unjustified. We'd wanted to get away from all the hype and publicity surrounding the cup and prepare quietly, but we failed in that anyway when a photographer discovered Jonah Lomu there with his girlfriend. So much for peace and quiet. We had to be somewhere in the days before the quarterfinal. Why not the south of France? It may sound exotic to New Zealanders at home who have never travelled, but All Blacks — and Super 12 players — know that the glamour of travel and faraway places soon palls.

We still trained while we were in France, we still had meetings, but the break was refreshing for us. It turned out to be a bit of a farce because of Jonah anyway and it was not ideal for either him or the team. We have sympathy for Jonah because none of us has had to put up with the intense spotlight that he's always under. On the one hand we're pleased because it takes the spotlight away from the rest of us but, on the other, it can be disruptive to us as a team. Of course the media couldn't care less about the equilibrium of the team — all they want is yet another photo or story of Jonah doing something, anything.

When we were up 24-10 against France after Jonah Lomu's second try four minutes into the second half, everything was going great. We didn't feel, or at least I didn't, that we had the match won then because that sort of thinking is fatal. But I did feel that we had control and if we just kept playing the way we were, we'd be fine. But we weren't.

The French found reserves of passion from somewhere and after the two dropped goals took them up to 24-16, they found a gear that we could not match. Maybe some of us as individual All Blacks didn't respond as we should have and maybe the All Blacks collectively don't play France often enough to know how they can play at times. The French had played like that before, coming from behind to beat better opponents, particularly against England in what was then the Five Nations, but the way they played at

185

What more needs to be said?

Twickenham that day was beyond the experience of most of the All Blacks.

In half an hour of rugby, the French did what they wanted to do and we couldn't. We didn't get the opportunity. For those minutes, they were better than us and that was when the lack of collective creativity in our outside backs showed. We didn't panic but neither could we put the moves together that we should have.

Our inability in those 30 minutes was elevated to the status of a failed campaign. We knew it came down to just what happened on the field but the public and the media saw it as much more than that. It was the climate that had been created.

The peripheral stuff like the marketing and publicity didn't affect us as players but it certainly seemed to have created an undue and unfair expectation of us. It was unfortunate that the first year of adidas as the New Zealand union's apparel supplier coincided with cup year. It revolutionised the marketing of the All Blacks. It was more aggressive world-wide as a marketer than Canterbury International had been and though adidas wasn't an official cup sponsor, its advertising and presence was much more widespread in Britain during the cup than any of the official sponsors. Their methods of publicity, the posters with the front row and that sort of stuff, created the image of us as being larger than life, of being invincible. We knew we weren't, but the public believed the hype rather than the reality.

As I've said, the higher we were pushed, the further the public had to fall and it was the All Blacks themselves who suffered.

It was devastating for us as players to lose that semifinal but the reaction from the New Zealand public and news media hurt much more. We'd lost a rugby game. Let's keep things in perspective. We'd lost a game that denied us the chance to win the World Cup. Few criminals convicted of the most heinous crimes, few politicians whose deeds have a daily impact on the lives of all New Zealanders, have been as vilified as much as we were and, in particular, as much as John Hart was.

From phone calls home and what we heard in that week between the semifinal and the playoff match, every All Black dreaded going home. The public thought the All Blacks had let them down. We thought the public, our greatest supporters, had let us down. In times of stress and when things aren't going well, it's a time to stick together, to support each other. But we felt as if we'd been cut adrift. We felt as All Blacks that we were pariahs in our own country.

Through us losing one game of rugby, it felt as if the reputation of the All Blacks, built up over so many years, had been destroyed by this one match and, judging from the reaction, as if we the players had willingly

It was a sad, lonely walk back to the Twickenham dressing room.

Photosport

187

gone along with that destruction.

We were even criticised, in the immediate aftermath of the semifinal, for not going back out on to Twickenham to applaud France. Applaud France? They'd just beaten us. Applauding them was the last thing on my mind and I'm sure that was the case for most of us. We were shattered. We slumped in the dressing room with an air of disbelief. There was no requirement on us to go back out and clap the French. It didn't cross my mind to do so. It may look good to manfully stride out, head held high, and clap the opposition, but that's just windowdressing, just gloss. The substance was that we were devastated. We had that awful sick feeling in the pit of the stomach and our hearts were breaking. It was France's day, not ours.

Our hearts were not in the playoff match the following Thursday. Taine Randell said so publicly and, from what I heard, was criticised for it. Taine could have been more tactful and diplomatic but if those New Zealanders who did the criticising can't handle honesty, perhaps the reaction said more about them than it did about Taine. That match has an unhappy history from each of the World Cups and it should be done away with. No one likes playing in it. When the first cup playoff match was held in Rotorua in 1987 and Wales beat Australia, the Australians didn't even bother to collect their third place trophy, their consolation prize. Don't administrators, and the public, understand that we're playing top level sport, that it's not a school sports in which the losers are rewarded so they don't get discouraged? When you go to win a tournament, playing to finish third or fourth means nothing.

The match against South Africa was a test match, though, and we did our best in Cardiff. The guys gave their all. But it was not realistic to expect any better from us.

The playoff match is a waste of time. It should be abolished. There's no point to it. It means nothing. Is that plain enough?

Ironically, it was in the Cardiff match that the outside backs returned to what I thought they always should have been, with Christian Cullen back at fullback and me on the wing. I'd told John Hart who I thought should be the backs and I expressed the concerns I had with his selections. I'm loath to criticise him because he thought he was doing what was best for the team, but my view was that the selection of Christian at centre was the team's downfall. At halftime in the match against South Africa, he expressed concern that we were kicking too much and I suggested that Christian should go back to fullback. When Pita Alatini replaced Tana Umaga at halftime, it was my call that Christian went back to where I thought he belonged and I went on the wing.

It's unfortunate that the All Blacks, technically anyway, now have to qualify for the next World Cup, but that's the fault of the rules, not the fault of the guys who played in Cardiff.

I'd already planned a European holiday with my mother after the cup so I didn't have to return home immediately and face the wrath of a country spurned. I'd chosen earlier to shelter myself from the reaction, win or lose.

I felt for guys such as John Hart and Taine Randell who had to return home and face the media and the public. That was their job, I know, but it wouldn't have been easy for them. Most of the criticism of them was not directed at them face to face in any case. There's nothing like a bit of moral courage when cloaked with anonymity. Or worse, people who say one thing to your face and something quite the opposite behind your back.

All Blacks can face a mirror with a clear conscience. Could the same be said of our detractors?

Any All Black accepts criticism as a part of the territory of being an All Black and if it's constructive criticism, no one minds. But the level of the attacks on the team as a whole, and on some individuals, degenerated into personal attacks and were quite disgusting. One radio broadcaster suggested on air that Taine should take his two degrees and shove them. That's the level to which reaction descended.

The result of the French match is reflected on the faces of John Hart, Wayne Smith and Peter Sloane.

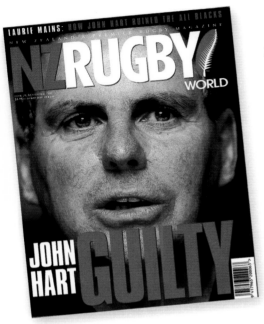

On the magazine cover:

LAURIE MAINS: HOW JOHN HART RUINED THE ALL BLACKS

NEW ZEALAND'S PREMIER RUGBY MAGAZINE

NZ RUGBY WORLD

JOHN HART GUILTY

The level to which some of our detractors descended.

The *NZ Rugby Monthly* magazine that had a photo of Hart on the cover with the single word "guilty" underneath was despicable. It was treating him much worse than any New Zealand newspaper or magazine treats any real criminals, much less a rugby coach whose team won far more than it lost.

Those same broadcasters and reporters rely on the players for interviews from All Blacks to help their ratings or sales. They rely on our goodwill and our sense of responsibility. A pity we cannot expect the same from them.

Of course John Hart has faults and who among us could honestly say we don't? And yes, he made mistakes during his time as All Black coach just as any human being makes mistakes.

There is an ugly, intolerant side to New Zealanders that surfaces occasionally and it is sad to see. It was evident in the reaction to the semifinal loss and it was evident again when John Hart went to Addington soon after his return home to watch a horse, of which he was a part-owner, run. A section of the crowd was crudely abusive to him and it shook him greatly. No man should have to put up with that, no New Zealander should be subject to such extremes of the worst of human behaviour, and especially not a man who had achieved things in his life to which his detractors could not even begin to aspire.

We New Zealanders, in our smug, secure, isolated part of the world, watch with lofty amusement crowds at soccer games in Europe or Latin America venting their anger at players, referees or their fellow spectators. We laugh about hot-blooded Latinos or speak with scorn about soccer yobbos who rampage through European city streets. We are passionate about our sport, we like to think, but we are also civilised. The reaction to the World Cup showed that sometimes we are no better.

Players hate losing — I detest it — but they know how to lose. They know how to accept defeat graciously and to accept victories with humility.

The public, as the World Cup showed, is not quite so good at it.

The public, through the voice of the media, used the excuse that the loss against France hurt them deeply. Not as much as the players were hurt, I can assure you.

12. Home is where the heart is

As the shadows from the setting sun were cast ever wider over Carisbrook on the late afternoon of 25 October 1998, I wondered if I could ever have a better day in rugby. Otago had just won the NPC first division title, beating a good Waikato side 49-20, and it was a special day for me personally and for the team.

It was the culmination of everything that Otago rugby meant to me. It's special for any team to win the NPC, whatever division it is, but for me an Otago victory was even more special.

It's not always easy to describe, this feeling of kinship and community that is Otago rugby. It's more than a football team — it's a whole way of life, a total environment and the players are just the centre of it. It's like throwing a stone into a pond. We're the stone that causes the reaction and the ripple upon ripple are the supporters, the city of Dunedin itself, wider Otago, everyone who is involved in Otago rugby and everyone who follows it. And, as players, we know the followers are by no means confined to the geographical area that is Otago. Wherever we go, wherever we play, there seems always to be someone, or a group of someones, dressed in blue and gold and with blue and gold faces and flags. It surely must have the greatest expatriate following of any provincial team in New Zealand.

Every team has its ethos or what modern coaches call its culture, ways of doing things, ways of behaving, a special bond between players wherever they may have been from originally. Otago has had a great many imported players over the years but it's never mattered what their origins were — what mattered was that they had become Otago people and they entered wholeheartedly into the Otago way of things.

I think if anyone ever wondered what was special about Otago rugby, they needed only to be in Dunedin the night of the final. It was a balmy night, which seemed altogether fitting, and Dunedin was a joyous place to be, even perhaps for Waikato supporters still vainly ringing their cowbells. Hundreds, perhaps thousands, stood around in the Octagon drinking in high good humour with not a hint of drink-induced trouble, and George Street was

191

Thanking our supporters at Carisbrook after winning the NPC. I join Brendon Timmins, Taine Randell and Carl Hoeft and, right, Taine and I pose with the prize.

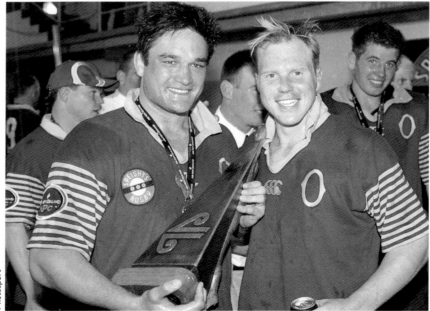

alive with traffic and people moving north or south, or to or from the scarfie area of North Dunedin. Strangers embraced strangers, Otago supporters embraced Waikato supporters, players were fêted.

I know, believe me, I know, that rugby supporters can be fickle and the old saying that you're only as good as your last game always holds true. But Otago supporters, or at least the hard core of them, are loyal throughout — they, like the players, have been through the bad times and it makes the good times all that more noteworthy.

Otago was a great place to be on that day in 1998 and I wouldn't have had it any other way. I'd had offers to play elsewhere and it didn't matter what money was being talked about, I was never going. Physically, I was in Otago but even more compelling was that I was mentally and spiritually in Otago always. Some things are just unwavering in my attitude and that is one of them. Money-hungry people have told me I was stupid, that I could have named my own price to go somewhere else. Maybe I could have, but I also had to have self-respect and I would never have had that if I'd gone somewhere just for the sake of a few more dollars.

Loyalty has always been a key factor for me. It was bred into me and I would never sacrifice it for anything. People told me that when I finished playing, no one would remember me so I may as well make as much capital out of playing as I could. What they don't consider is that I have to remember myself, I have to live with myself for the rest of my life. That was why I could never turn my back on Otago. It's the loyalty and self-respect that is the essence of being an Otago player.

What made winning the NPC in 1998 even more special was that we had a good team that was playing very well, sublimely on occasions. The win in the final, 49-20, was impressive enough, but look at some of the other scores we achieved that year: Northland, 84-10. Wellington, 82-10. Southland, 60-10 (with uncontested scrums for the second half). North Harbour, 39-8. Taranaki, 61-12.

I think the Wellington game at Carisbrook was probably the most perfect rugby I've been involved in with any Otago team. We demolished them. We knew we were a special team and we went out with the intention of smashing them, knowing that we'd smash them. It was an incredible feeling and one that doesn't come often to a rugby player. It was a feeling of utter dominance, of total control of the game from the opening whistle.

The way the 1998 All Black season had panned out was also a factor in Otago's success. There were an increasing number of us in the All Black team and as the test losses accumulated, we just wanted to get back into the environment that we knew and understood, away from the instability and away from the suffocating expectations that the All Blacks always had to win. It wasn't that the Otago All Blacks talked about this, it was just an

**Overleaf:
Scoring against
Wellington — probably
the most perfect rugby
I've been involved in
with any Otago team.
We won 82-10.**

193

unspoken feeling that we all shared. Some felt a lot more comfortable in the Otago environment than they had with the All Blacks. We wanted to get back to enjoying our rugby again and we knew we were good enough to win. Walking back into the Otago dressing room was like arriving home after a time away, back to the familiar surroundings, the friends and family.

Some of us rejoined Otago for the fourth match of the NPC, against Counties-Manukau, and some for the fifth, against Auckland. We should never have lost that match at Eden Park. We were up early and then made silly mistakes and took wrong options to let them back in and, in the way that Auckland seems to be able to do better than other teams, they galloped away from us. As a result, some doubts crept into the Otago team but we collectively decided we had to be more dynamic and attack more frequently, hitting opponents with the unexpected. Auckland did us a favour because they, unwittingly, showed us the path to the final.

Holding that NPC trophy aloft — I think all the team had a go at holding it up — was one of the most satisfying moments of my rugby life. If only I'd been able to do the same with the World Cup.

There are many elements to the Otago way. Some of the intensity of comradeship comes about because of the heritage, the traditions of Otago rugby, especially the times before and after the Second World War when the Ranfurly Shield never moved north of the Waitaki. These were the days of the great Otago-Southland matches, when Carisbrook or Rugby Park in Invercargill were packed and when special trains would travel north or south jammed with supporters. This was when Vic Cavanagh coached Otago and the era culminated in 11 Otago players being in the All Blacks in South Africa in 1949. Modern players such as myself don't know the details of this history, but we're well aware of its broad sweep and the impact that Otago then had on New Zealand rugby, and the impact that rugby had on Otago.

Succeeding generations absorbed what had gone before and created their own layers of history and when I arrived on the scene, it was the end of the nine years of Laurie Mains being coach, during which Otago had won the NPC in 1991 and had developed a reputation for muscling their way through games that gradually evolved, in Laurie's latter years, into an exciting brand of fast, high-risk, attacking rugby. This continued under Gordon Hunter when I became involved. There have always been dominant players, guys who are around longer than others, and they absorb, adhere to and then pass on the Otago way of doing things to the players that follow them. In the late 80s there were players such as Greg Cooper, Steve Hotton, Dave Latta, Richard Knight, Brent Pope, Mike Brewer, John Timu, Jamie Joseph, Arran Pene — any number really — and the guys who succeeded them, and who willingly bought into the ethos, were people such as John Leslie, Brendon

Timmins, Marc Ellis, Josh Kronfeld, Taine Randell and then me. We were carrying the torch for the new generation and we knew that we had a tradition to uphold and a responsibility to ensure that Otago rugby was in as good heart when we left as it was when we arrived.

David Latta perhaps best sums up the Otago attitude. The reason people play football is to play alongside guys such as David Latta. His level of commitment and his desire and passion for Otago rugby are as great as mine. There wouldn't be any player in New Zealand who did not respect him.

As players arrive from outside the area, they bring different perspectives and outlooks and the differences are encouraged, so long as they're brought within the team, the close-knit family that is Otago rugby. We don't restrict anyone's ability to be themselves — and Marc Ellis is probably a prime example of that — but we do expect them to wholeheartedly embrace what we're doing. The team comes first. Always.

Marc Ellis deserves a special mention because he's as mad as a cut snake. He's invaluable to any team not because of his antics, but because of his enthusiasm for playing the game.

Passion and pride in the faces, happiness too after beating South Africa in 1994. Jamie Joseph, David Latta and Paul Cooke and I savour the moment.

No need to say where this photo was taken. The Carisbrook terrace, of course!

Within Otago there is an element, not as prevalent as it once was, of varsity antics, of boys being boys within Otago, and that too is part of the team-building exercise. Senior players, the boys in the back seat of the bus, used to be able to order the new guys to do almost anything, and they'd have to do it before they'd be accepted. Some things are best not published, but I don't think Marc Ellis would mind me relating the story of his initiation when he was a fresh-faced scarfie down from Wellington. He was required to strip naked and move from the back of the bus to the front along the luggage rack that ran along the side above the seats.

My initiation was altogether more prosaic. I had to drink a jug of beer. When rugby players are told to "do a jug", that doesn't mean leisurely sipping from a glass with an elbow on the bar over half an hour or so. It means to drink from the jug continuously and it is not allowed to be removed from the mouth. I didn't drink at all in those days but I manfully swallowed my rite of passage, not attempting to match the speed-drinking records of some of my teammates who can put jugs away at an astonishing rate.

Lest some prurient wowser is reading this, let me say that these things very seldom get out of hand and if there's even a hint of something going a bit far, there's always someone who will call a halt. It's all harmless, good fun.

"Doing a jug" is not as common now as it once was, but there still is a time when it is mandatory. Among the most successful sports sponsorships has been the Speight's sponsorship of Otago rugby. We value what Speight's does for the team and for the union — probably much more than its contract requires — and in turn we are loyal to Speight's. Woe betide any player who is caught, knowingly or otherwise, drinking any competing brewer's products, which are generally known within Otago as the devil's urine. Any player so caught is immediately ordered to do a jug (of Speight's of course) in order to flush the body of the offending fluid. This is most likely to happen when we're away and in foreign territory, such as Canterbury or Auckland, which are sponsored by another brewery. Speight's can't be had for love or money at Jade Stadium or Eden Park and some players find the need for a beer after the game just too tempting. Inevitably, they pay the price.

This is not to suggest that the Otago ethos is centred on drinking. It is not. Its focus is family, the immediate family of the team and the wider family of relatives and friends, union staff, administrators and supporters. Loyalty to the cause is the key, whatever the circumstances.

The liaison with Speight's has also brought Otago, in the last few years, its own song which seems to epitomise what Otago means to all who are a part of it. It's *Southern Man* (written by an Aucklander of all things) which espouses the things we hold dear such as loyalty, comradeship, ruggedness, the southern attitude of independence, the underdog status, a touch of conservatism . . . all of those things with which we identify ourselves and things which others attribute to us. Anyone at the NPC final in 1998 would have seen and felt for themselves the impact the song had when it was sung to the crowded terrace by a local entertainer, Denis Henderson, and it's been adopted as our team song. We usually sing it in the dressing room after games and the new boys only have to read the words a couple of times before they chuck them away and sing it from the heart. Invariably, the guitar accompaniment is provided by Brendan Laney, another "import" who has immersed himself totally in the Otago way (though being from South Canterbury, he didn't have to travel far).

I don't suppose the copyright holders will mind too much if I repeat the words here which tell the story better than I can:

Some of the boys,
Got it into their heads,
'bout moving up north,
To follow the bread.
That ain't for me,
That kind of thing just don't rate,
This is one Southern boy,
Who ain't crossing the Strait.

Now I might not be rich,
But I like things down here,
We got the best looking girls,
And the best damn beer.
So you can keep your Queen City,
With your cocktails and cool,
Give me a beer in a seven,
With the boys shooting pool.

I'm a Southern Man,
Well, I'm Southern bred,
I got the South in my blood,
And I'll be here till I'm damn well dead.

'Cause here we just know,
What makes a Southern boy tick,
And it ain't margaritas,
With some fruit on a stick.
Well it might not be fancy,
But when you come from down here.
We know you got the best girl,
And you got the best beer.

I'm a Southern Man etc etc.

The song seems to express what we're about. All teams I imagine have their own ethos, their own way of doing things and their own special traits, and the Southern Man and the Otago way is us. Being an All Black, I could see the differences with guys from other teams and initially they would bring their provincial way of doing things into the All Blacks. It was the job of the coach and senior players to mould the All Blacks' own ethos, based of course on the very successful playing record, so that it wasn't a mirror of Auckland or Otago or any other province. Sometimes, I understand, this hadn't worked all that well in the All Blacks and one province dominated the others, with the players from that province calling the shots. This could lead to cliques within the wider squad and would be fatal to the team spirit.

Another area where the All Blacks differ is that they don't have a home town or a home ground the way all provinces do, so the feeling of community that Otago, for example, has, doesn't apply in the All Blacks. It is nationalism rather than provincialism that drives us in the All Blacks, plus the other factors such as personal satisfaction, achieving goals and the like.

Dunedin is central to the Otago rugby way, not just because that's where the team is based but because of the type of city it is. It is a rugby city, its people are proud of its rugby team and rugby is very much central to the wellbeing of Dunedin and Otago. Dunedin is relatively small and therefore most players are fairly well known and we couldn't walk anonymously down George Street the way some Auckland players, for example, might be able to walk down Queen Street. But Dunedin people are very supportive and it's very rare for any of the players to be given a hard time. Occasionally we might get a nod or a "G'day Jeff" but we don't get pestered. Dunedin people give us the space we need and it's a very supportive environment.

I'm constantly amazed that people who've never lived in Dunedin can call it a boring city. I've never found it so and, in fact, it's quite the opposite that keeps players in Dunedin once they arrive from somewhere else. We've had players come down somewhat reluctantly because they've heard talk about cold weather and that there's nothing to do in Dunedin, but within a week of arriving they're raving about the place. Some never leave, even when they've finished playing.

It's not everyone who can adapt to life as a Southern Man, however. An exception to the normal rule was Glen Ross, who became coach of Otago in 1996 when Gordon Hunter became an All Black selector. I think he was the first person from outside the area to coach Otago and while that was known at the time, it was thought that he, like all the players who move south, would soon adapt. After all, he did have a Scottish-sounding name so he was halfway there.

But Glen, I'm sorry to say, didn't fit in as well as we all thought or hoped he would, and he had two fairly uncomfortable years in Dunedin. It was far from being all his fault and rather than attribute blame at all, I think it's fair to say simply that Glen Ross and Otago rugby just didn't click. That happens sometimes in sport, just as it does in business I suppose when someone is hired to do a job but who doesn't turn out to be exactly what was required.

Overleaf, left:
Mixing it with
Carlos Spencer at
Carisbrook during a
Super 12 match in 1999.

Overleaf, right:
Scoring against the
Auckland Blues in the
Super 12 semifinal at
Eden Park in 1998.

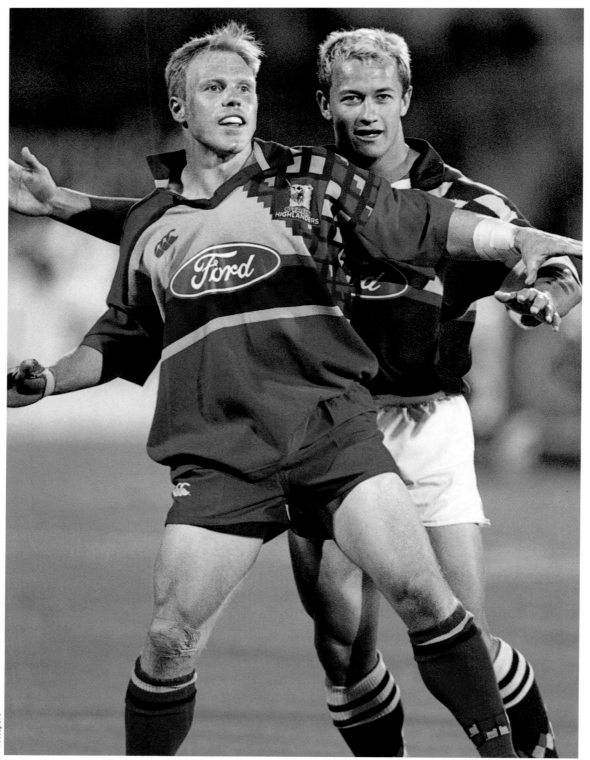

203

Through no particular fault of anyone, the mix just didn't work.

Ross also had a difficult job of more or less rebuilding Otago rugby which, over the summer of 1995-96, had lost senior players such as Jamie Joseph, Arran Pene and John Timu, and others such as David Latta who was in the twilight of his career. It was also the dawn of a new rugby era with players being paid for the first time and the introduction of the Super 12. It would have been a difficult time for any coach, no matter how gifted and no matter where he was from.

Ross had had a fairly successful tenure as the Waikato coach but that's a totally different environment to Otago and while coaches now freely move from one area to another, his inability to perform as expected showed that adapting to a different culture is a key requirement for a coach, just as it is for a player.

He was technically very good but perhaps his one major drawback, other than not being from Otago, was that he didn't have that hard edge that coaches sometimes need. He was articulate and he put his points of view forcefully but too often he either couldn't or wouldn't follow through with the required hard action. A coach has to have the ability to intimidate players if necessary the way Laurie Mains did, but Glen Ross wasn't able to do that.

I personally didn't have a problem with Ross, and I seldom have had with any coach, but some players lost respect for him and that's fatal in a rugby team. He often changed his mind about selections or what he wanted of us and, as a result, we didn't have much security as a team and we were often confused about precisely what was required of us. It got to the stage where we decided that if we were to enjoy our rugby — and what's the point in playing if you don't enjoy it? — we'd have to play the way we wanted to and not the way we were being directed to.

Dunedin being a small, close-knit city, it doesn't take too long for these sorts of things to get around and that, coupled with some poor performances, led to the Otago union questioning Ross' ability. As players, we didn't get involved in the politics of the game but we were certainly aware of what was going on and we found it very difficult to support him when we knew he wasn't getting support from the union.

A rugby team can too often be seen in isolation from everything else. The team comprises the players who do the work on the field but behind them are a lot of people who work for the team in various ways and it was clear during 1997 that some were pulling in different directions and that had an effect on the team.

Ross found himself in an increasingly untenable situation and eventually, early in 1998, he and the Otago union reached agreement on his departure and Tony Gilbert was appointed in his place, first for the Highlanders and then for Otago. I felt sorry for Glen but felt also that it was the best move for Otago and the players. How good it was quickly became apparent when we made the Super 12 semifinals for the first time in Tony's first year and won the NPC that year.

Tony Gilbert, a real Southern Man who had the knack of seeing the overall picture as well as being able to relate to individual players, was the coach who made it all happen and he fully deserved to be promoted to the All Black panel after just two years with the Highlanders, and only one with Otago. It helped Tony immensely that he had coached the University A and Kaikorai clubs, as well as being assistant Otago coach to Gordon Hunter, so that he knew most of the players intimately and with some, such as Josh Kronfeld and Taine Randell, he had been involved with them since they'd first moved to Dunedin to go to university. It gave him an advantage that Glen Ross could never have had.

For all that, I believe Glen did some good things while he was in Dunedin and, in particular, much of the rapid rise by our front row of Kees Meeuws, Anton Oliver and Carl Hoeft was due in large measure to the work that Glen put into them.

Glen did the best possible job he could but he just wasn't the right man for the job. He tried very hard to adapt to Otago but in the end he failed and that's the way coaches are judged. It can be a harsh world.

It was during Glen's time that I played what a lot of people said was my best game of rugby. That was for Otago against Wellington at Athletic Park and came at the stage when the players had decided they had to take things into their own hands. Personally, I was going through a phase where I wasn't particularly enjoying the rugby and I was just making the best of it I could. Leading into that Wellington game, we hadn't had a very good preparation and we weren't feeling very comfortable at all about our ability. It was also another rotten day, one that we seemed to strike a lot at Athletic Park.

The Mike Gibson Memorial Trophy was at stake again and that always brings out the best in Otago teams while it seems to be strangely undervalued by Wellington teams. We played for the trophy and we played as if we had

Top left:
Glen Ross ... not
the right man.

Bottom left:
Tony Gilbert ... a real
Southern Man.

nothing to lose. We'd been erratic until that game but then in the Athletic Park wind and rain everything seemed to come right. The team played superbly and although I was happy with the way I played, it just happened that I was in the right place at the right times. That's the way it is sometimes and while I was flattered with all the comment after the game about how "Jeff Wilson" had beaten Wellington, that game showed how much of a team game rugby really is. I was able to dominate because of the work done by my teammates. If they hadn't fired as well, no one would have heard of me.

The Wellington game and the final match of the year three weeks later against Canterbury at Carisbrook gave us the chance to show that, even in adverse conditions, we could be a very capable team. Those two wins were very heartening for us — and for our supporters — and were good indicators for what happened the following year when we were the best team in the competition.

Even when things weren't going all that well, the Otago ethos got us through. It is a very powerful force for the players.

When Tony Gilbert — The Grandfather as he was known — arrived, there was a new buzz within the team. He was someone who had been involved with Otago rugby, he'd been a sort of an overseer when Gordon Hunter was the coach, and he had a vast knowledge of the game. He was someone who had bided his time and waited for his opportunities.

Tony was the sort of coach who was always in control, who never seemed flummoxed by anything. Rather than have favourites among the players, as some coaches do, all the players were his favourites. There was no doubting that he was the boss. There was no questioning his decisions — it was his way or the highway.

His job was to mould a team that would be the nucleus of Otago and Highlanders teams for some years to come. All teams are built on their front rows and we had one. We also had youth and talent in the loose forwards and the tight five, previously an Otago weakness, was now our strength. As a result, Tony had the unenviable task of changing the Otago way of playing — from a team that lived off scraps of possession and attacked from everywhere to compensate, to a team that began its work up front and gradually tired opponents into submission.

For all the talent we had available, and the confidence that comes from winning, Tony somehow always managed to confirm in our minds the idea that we were the underdogs, and Otago teams always perform best when they think their backs are to the wall. By doing that, he also ensured that we had our feet firmly on the ground.

Making the semifinals in the Super 12 that year — losing to the Auckland Blues in a game which, with a bit more luck, we could have won — confirmed for us all that the NPC was ours for the taking providing that we continued to follow the Gilbert line.

And so it proved. Gilbert was the team's head off the field and John Leslie was the team's heart on it. Every team needs a player such as "JL", someone who acts as the lieutenant to the captain, someone who is the players' player, and John Leslie was that man for the Highlanders and Otago in 1998. He has the heart and soul of a genuine rugby player who would never let his team down. His standards were so high that he could not tolerate mediocrity in preparation or in playing and he was so intense at times about his rugby that he was mistaken for being laidback. It was a pleasure to play with someone such as "JL" who made the most of his ability.

After John left for Scotland, Anton Oliver stepped easily and naturally into the able lieutenant's role.

The tackle ball law made life difficult for us in the 1999 Super 12, as it undoubtedly did for all the other teams. It's a law that has often caused confusion but the main difficulty for us was that it negated to a certain extent the influence that Josh Kronfeld could have on a game. Under the law operating in 1999, players could join a tackle from any position and with an arbitrary time set for release of the ball, "tackle situations" as referees like to call them, became just a lottery. That affected the way we played but our attitude was a factor too. We seemed to coast along until we knew we had to win. We won some games that we weren't even in for

Anton Oliver ... the able lieutenant.

much of the time and other times we'd come off the field feeling as if we hadn't even played. The final against the Crusaders was a prime example of that. We were tired after returning from the semifinal against the Stormers in Cape Town, but we should have been better than we were. I recall late in the game a realisation seemed to jolt the players into action: "Hell, we could lose this game." By then, it was too late.

Josh Kronfeld, more than any other player, was associated with the various changes to the tackle ball laws. Television commentators would say things such as, "If Josh can't understand it, no one can." Of course, if you ask Josh, he never gave away a penalty in his whole career. In fact, he became New Zealand's best referee since the retirement of Sean Fitzpatrick.

Josh was an individual who was a very proud All Black but for whom rugby was only one facet of a diverse career and life. He was absolutely reckless on the rugby field and had no regard for his body

Photosport

207

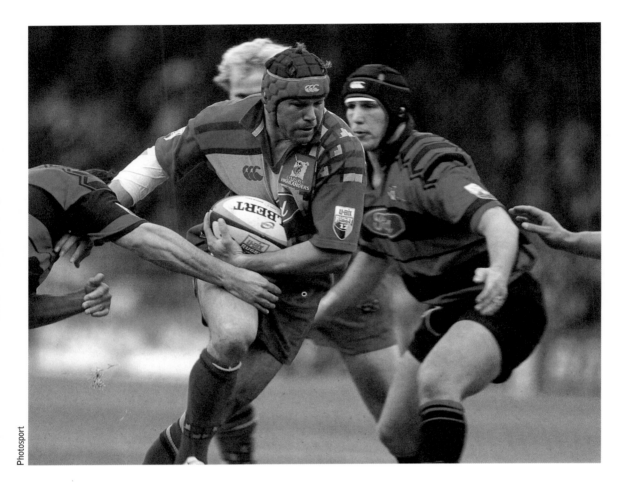

Superb rugby is just one of Josh Kronfeld's diverse interests.

whatsoever, as any number of doctors and physios could testify.

Tony Gilbert has a huge challenge now as assistant coach of the All Blacks and, by the time this is read, we will know the results of the domestic tests and of the tri-nations. He will have found the All Blacks a totally different environment to what he was used to: there would have been vastly more pressure to perform and it will have been interesting to observe how he's handled the expectations of the media and the public and the fact that the All Blacks can never be the underdog. For a change, I will have done my observing from the outside.

The All Blacks are not truly Tony's team — they're Wayne Smith's team — but knowing Tony, he will have made his feelings clear when he felt the need. If anyone could earn the respect of the players and of the public, it would be Tony.

With Tony Gilbert's fast-tracked departure to the All Blacks, the Highlanders had to find another coach, and again, the administrators turned to someone from outside the area, Peter Sloane.

This was welcome news to the Otago players who were with the All Blacks, where Peter had been assistant coach. When I first heard that he was going to the Highlanders, I was driving around the North Island and I phoned him to tell him how pleased I was. I was echoing the thoughts of other All Blacks who knew that Peter had operated in difficult circumstances with the New Zealand team and that he deserved the chance to have a team of his own.

I don't think there was any other coach who could have handled the team at such short notice. Peter's biggest difficulty was taking a team that he hadn't selected — that had been done by Tony Gilbert before he knew he would be involved with the All Blacks. But with the typical let's-get-on-with-it attitude of a former hooker, Peter accepted what he had and just totally immersed himself in his new role.

He brought with him the hard-nosed approach of a former All Black front-rower but he also, through his All Black involvement, had the advantage of all the technological skills. His knowledge of the game could never be questioned and he brought with him also genuine concern for the welfare of the players. Not just concern about how they play the game or how they train for it, but about what else they do. Outside of rugby, Peter was a successful builder with his own company and he was coaching because of his love for the game, not for the money. I think that says a lot about him.

Without him, I would have got out of rugby sooner than I did. I doubt that I would have finished the Super 12. His understanding of how I felt and of what I wanted to do helped me get through to the end of the Super 12 and even to see some light at the end of the sporting tunnel.

Though an outsider in an Otago sense, he seemed to have no trouble adjusting. The fact he'd been with the Crusaders for two years was an advantage in terms of looking at the world through South Island eyes and moving to Dunedin just dropped him deeper in the culture of the Southern Man. It was at his behest that every member of the Highlanders squad — players and management — had to have in their cars and play cassettes or CDs of the *Southern Man* and the Highlanders songs.

I was disappointed for Peter that the Highlanders didn't do better than they did in 2000, but the fact was it was not an easy season for him or the players. Our team just didn't suit the style of the competition. Injuries dogged us at crucial times and we never really had a solid squad of 26. A prime factor was that we had no one in the backline over 95 kg while other teams had guys of 100-plus. That was a big difference. We also lost speed outside with injuries to Rico Gear and Dan Parkinson and we lost Taine Randell for five weeks after he'd been playing sensational football.

Taine had been injured in the Cats game and was being treated and couldn't front up for the mandatory Sky interviews. So I was asked to step

**Peter Sloane ... a
Northerner who quickly
became a Southern Man.**

into the breach and I was pleased that being interviewed at the same time was Chester Williams, one of the genuine nice guys of the game. I always enjoyed playing against him because he was a good player with a lot of heart and because he was always a good challenge.

I believe not having Isitolo Maka was a big loss. Admittedly, he had not had a great NPC the previous year but I believe he would have made the step up required of him. His size and intimidation would have been important to us and his absence was compounded by not having his replacement, Paul Miller, for a time because of injury. Another crucial player from the previous year who was missing was Brian Lima.

We had the forwards and we could have been dominant given the right forward platform, but the backs were not able to give them all the go-forward that they needed.

I don't want this to sound like a catalogue of excuses because it's not, but we also had the toughest road season of all, playing all the Highlanders' bogey teams away — the Crusaders, Blues, the Waratahs and the Brumbies.

For all that, there were good aspects to the Super 12. We did make the semifinals, which eight other teams didn't do, we had Anton Oliver and, before his injury, Taine Randell in superb form, we had Simon Maling step up to be one of the great improvers of the year, and we had the exciting promise of Samiu Vahafolau.

It was, in the end, a disappointing season, but not without hope. That is a commodity Otago teams always have.

13. G-force

Lynne Wilson

It's not often that Jeffrey — I suppose mothers like to stick with the names they gave their children — can relax and be himself. That's a price that he and others pay for their status in sport or, I imagine, in any other field that gives them instant recognition wherever they go. Us ordinary people can barely imagine what it's like to be a public face all the time where every move is watched, examined and analysed.

I had an insight into this after the World Cup in 1999 when Jeffrey and I went on one of those bus tours of Europe, the "today's Tuesday so it must be Belgium" sort of trip. We'd planned it long before the cup and we both looked forward to it, me because I'd never travelled extensively in Europe and because it gave me a chance to be with Jeffrey for a few weeks, and he because it gave him a chance to relax after the cup, whatever the result.

There had been plans for victory parades in New Zealand and all the All Blacks were told they'd have to go straight home after the cup. If Jeffrey's views were representative of those of the other players, none of them would have liked the talk of the parades. It was all very well to plan victory parades, but first you have to have the victory. It was a quiet Jeffrey whom I picked up from, of all places, the hotel in Cardiff where the Australian team was staying. He was wearing a cap and had it pulled down, covering as much of his face as he could.

We went to the lovely Cotswolds town of Burton-on-the-Water for a few days before joining our bus tour of Europe and there we just relaxed, reading and wandering around. Jeffrey went to London for a couple of days to be with Josh Kronfeld who was playing the harmonica with Midge Marsden and others, but otherwise he just relaxed in the Cotswolds too. A day or so after the World Cup final, we were walking through the town when we saw coming toward us the Australian coach, Rod Macqueen, and what we took to be his family. Small world eh? We stopped and chatted and Jeffrey

Otago Daily Times

A lonely spectator ... and a proud Mum. Lynne Wilson in the stand at Carisbrook during the New Zealand-Australia youth test in 1993. This was taken when Jeff took his sixth wicket.

congratulated him on their victory, and Rod was very gracious. I'm sure he knew how Jeffrey was hurting inside.

The European tour was supposed to be a time for mother and son to be together and to enjoy ourselves and it turned out too to be a chance for Jeffrey to try to forget about rugby for a while and to put the disappointment of the cup behind him — as much as he or any of the All Blacks could ever do that.

I don't think Jeffrey could travel incognito in many places in the world and he certainly couldn't on our trip. We'd barely joined the tour when an Australian woman sitting behind us recognised him and she couldn't wait until the next stop to find a cybercafé to email her friends and relatives. "Guess who's on the bus?" You can imagine the tone of the message. It soon got around the rest of the bus and for a day or two there was a bit of talking behind hands and pointing but after that they all settled down and accepted Jeffrey as another tourist, just like them.

It didn't stop the occasional ribbing, though, and the questions about what went wrong for the All Blacks. *Waltzing Matilda* got a fair old airing on the bus, I think a lot of it for our benefit, but Jeffrey just slunk down in his seat and didn't join in. His standard response to questions about the World Cup was, "We just weren't good enough, that's all."

One day on the bus Jeffrey had had enough of *Waltzing Matilda* and the Aussies — though they were all good-natured about it — and he jumped up, stood in the aisle, took his jacket off and did the haka. It was very impressive. I'd never been so close to anyone doing the haka before and I'm sure no one else in the bus had been either. It sent a shiver down my spine. Of course, that became the talk of the group and some of them were disappointed that they'd missed what one of the Canadian women on the bus called "that crazy dance". They wanted an encore but Jeffrey refused to oblige until, on the last night in Paris, he did it again. They all loved it and appreciated Jeffrey all the more for it. They were lost for words. All they knew about the haka was that it was the "dance" the All Blacks did before tests. And now here was one of the All Blacks doing it just for them!

I was delighted to have Jeffrey to myself for those weeks. It was the first time I'd been away with him since he was very young because sport took him on his own trips from an early age. It was a wonderful time and, for the most part, we were just another mother and son like so many other mothers and sons or mothers and daughters on the trip. We gave some of them nicknames — one family we called the Waltons and another, of teenage girls, we called the Spice Girls, one of whom we reckoned had been shouted a trip around Europe by her Daddy. A sort of finishing school. There was a priest from Dubbo in New South Wales and we called him Father Ted.

Jeffrey also earned a nickname from me. He spent so much time between travelling looking for phones and he once used a phone box that he found halfway up a mountain near Innsbruck. After that, I called him Clark — for Clark Kent.

Jeffrey wasn't all that good in the mornings. He'd get on the bus, slump down in his seat, pull his hat down and say, "Don't wake me till morning tea." But, after that, he was fine and we were just a couple more tourists really. I don't know though if many tourists would have got up to what Jeffrey did in our rooms. We shared rooms — and some of them were tiny — but Jeffrey still did his exercises and his weight training. He'd be there, dressed only in his Calvin Kleins and socks, using my suitcase, the heavier of the two, as his weights.

Jeffrey seemed to strike up a particular rapport with our driver, a cheery Italian called Chiro. Jeffrey used to get CDs and tapes for Chiro to play, kidding him along about what was good and what was not, and occasionally Chiro sang himself, much to the delight of all the passengers.

We had a few days in Vancouver at the end of it all, then Portland in

Brother Richard and Jeff ham it up during a replay of one of their epic matches in the family home.

Oregon where we went to the Nike complex, and then to Fiji. It was a wonderful holiday and an idyllic way for Jeffrey to put the disappointment of the World Cup as far behind him as he could.

Growing up in Invercargill, he was an ideal son. But that, of course, is a biased mother speaking.

I'd met Bill at training college in Dunedin and we got to know each other well very quickly. It was an ideal match and it wasn't too long before our first son, Richard, was born. We moved back to Invercargill through Bill's job and decided to wait a few years before another child and this turned out to be Jeffrey, born on 24 October 1973 — 10 lb 5 oz and three weeks overdue.

People have asked us if we'd have preferred a girl since we already had a boy but we didn't mind in the slightest, as long as he was fit and healthy, that was all that mattered.

It didn't seem too many years later that we realised just how fit and healthy Jeffrey was. Other than doing what all kids do, playing around with footballs and cricket bats and tennis racquets when they're very young, Jeffrey began competitive sport when he was about seven. I think it was probably at that very early age that Bill realised that Jeffrey was someone special in sport and within a couple of years he used to joke about one day being Jeffrey's manager and carrying his bags around the world. At that stage, it was cricket that was mostly talked about for the future because Bill was such a keen cricketer and Richard and Jeffrey were following the same path. Bill had visions of walking through the gates at Lord's carrying Jeffrey's "coffin".

I gave up very early being involved in the boys' sporting lives. That was

Bill's domain and I was left to go and do my own thing, playing tennis mostly. I think those early years were critical to Jeffrey's learning of not so much how the games were played, but of attitudes and the ethos of the games. He and Richard were always around the older men, listening and watching without saying much, and I'm sure everything they heard and saw was absorbed for later use.

Sport was always a significant part of their lives, but not the only part. Bill and I insisted that schoolwork had to come first and Jeffrey and Richard always knew that before they could go out to play or whatever, the homework had to be done. Jeffrey was a naturally bright kid and of all the years he was at school, neither Bill nor I once had to go to see a teacher to talk about Jeffrey's marks or his application or, thank goodness, his behaviour. He probably could have done better at school — that sounds as if it's written for a report card — but he was always above average and didn't have to struggle to get through. He'd set his heart on being a teacher and began at the College of Education in Dunedin before sport took over his life completely. I think he'd be a very good teacher, though, because he has a

Competition was intense here too – Mum, Dad, Richard and Jeff playing 500 at home in Invercargill.

Barry Harcourt/Southland Times

good manner about him and interacts particularly well with children.

We were, in a monetary sense, probably an average family, neither rich nor poor. Like a lot of families, we made do. Whenever the boys were away, they'd be given spending money of $2 a day — Richard always took full advantage and came home with nothing, but canny Jeffrey would always have something left. The money needed for the sports equipment and the trips was found somehow and we were lucky that I had a very generous mother, Grace Robertson, who helped out when asked. We had a strict rule of thumb that the boys had to be helped equally. Both boys later stayed in Dunedin with Grace at different times and I think she particularly enjoyed being Jeffrey's "minder" when public interest in him began to increase. I think she secretly liked the hype but she was never afraid to say no to anyone asking something of Jeffrey and sometimes she'd ring me and say, "You'll never guess what I told . . . "

Without a doubt, the person with the largest influence on Jeffrey's career was his father and I think he was particularly lucky to have someone like Bill who, while a father and therefore someone to be trusted without exception, also had such a good understanding of sport and an astute mind. I wonder how many other very talented young sports people are lost to sport because they don't have access to the same sort of guidance.

Bill had a bubbly, likeable personality and he liked to get thoroughly involved in everything, whatever it may have been. He was never in doubt that Jeffrey as a sportsman was something exceptional and he saw that at such an early age and was able to properly channel it while at the same time ensuring that he always played for enjoyment and tried whatever he wanted.

Later, when Jeffrey was an All Black and had played cricket for New Zealand, Bill's roles were various — father of course, and friend, counsellor and also business manager. Bill's astute brain always found the best course for Jeffrey, leaving him free to concentrate solely on the playing side of things, though Bill continued to advise him on that as well.

By that stage, Bill was manager of Briscoes in Invercargill and I'm sure his work days comprised 60 per cent of Jeff's business and 40 per cent of Briscoes'. I'm sure they won't mind me saying that, not that they didn't know because there was always a stream of people going into the store seeking Bill's advice or assistance. He was very happy with what he was doing, with the way his life had turned out.

He had the happy knack of knowing what was good and what was not so good for Jeffrey and deciding accordingly and if Jeffrey sometimes disagreed, if there was something he didn't want to do, Bill was always able to turn him around. Bill was pretty crafty — he could talk Jeffrey into doing something without Jeffrey knowing he'd been talked into it. Sometimes, he might have even thought it was his idea!

With the advent of Richard Reid from Nike and David Howman, the lawyer, the three of them were an ideal group to guide and advise Jeffrey and look after his interests.

For all Jeffrey's success and for all the money he's made doing what he enjoyed doing, I feel it is a tough life he leads. It's only people who lead a similar lifestyle who truly understand how little privacy there is and how abnormal the life really is. Most if not all of Jeffrey's friends from school have married, have children, have careers that will take them through until they're 60 or 65, they've been on overseas holidays and some of them have done the big OE, working and living in Australia or Europe for three or four years. Jeffrey hasn't had the opportunity for any of these things and while the opposite view might be that he's famous and that he's moderately wealthy, there still is a need for a "normal" life.

I think that's one of the reasons why Jeffrey likes to be alone at times. He just wants to be himself and not be "the public" Jeff Wilson that everyone either knows or wants to know.

The constant attention and recognition must get to people in these situations, but I'm always surprised how well Jeffrey handles himself when he's accosted by people in the street or in a restaurant or whatever. He's always polite and he always has something to say, but I know that he's also holding back a little of himself. Sometimes he's been accused of arrogance and I think that's grossly unfair and the accusations come from people who don't know him at all. What people see as arrogance is confidence, confidence in his ability as an athlete and also in his ability to handle whatever life dishes up to him. Confidence and arrogance are two entirely different things but I admit they can be confused from a distance.

The only time I've known him to get really angry about his public role was at the time of the gay rumours, and especially after a *Woman's Day* reporter phoned me and asked me for an interview, but didn't say why. I had a call from Jeffrey in Christchurch and I told him about the call and he was furious and went and tore a strip off the reporter, telling her what he thought.

Until then, I had been oblivious to the rumours. I learned later that they'd been flying around but no one ever said anything to me. I think people were trying to protect me from them. The magazine even tried to get to one of Jeffrey's former girlfriends, who was then in London. Her mother phoned me and asked what was going on.

I laughed it off when I heard about it. It was a hurtful time, though, made the more hurtful because there was not the slightest truth in it all.

I was never a great reader of *Woman's Day* before that and I'm certainly not now. I even cancelled our subscription to *Rugby News* after it repeated the rumour. It leapt to Jeffrey's defence but it should never have written a thing.

Those rumours were part of the price, I suppose, of being well known, although I had hoped that New Zealanders were above that sort of thing.

Aside from the *Woman's Day* and *Rugby News* episodes, Jeffrey tried to laugh the rumours off but I know that they got to him and I'm sure they confirmed in his mind that the sporting part of Jeff Wilson may be regarded as public property, but the private life is not and never should be.

No one knows Jeffrey better than me and what I can say, what I'm pleased to be able to say, is that for all his sporting prowess and for all his achievements and fame, he remains the lovable, loving, unaffected son he always has been.

Pro Sport Photos

Donny Cameron

(Donny Cameron has been the masseur for the Otago team since 1988, with the Highlanders since their inception and was with the All Blacks at the World Cup in 1995 and on their tour of Italy and France.)

Of all the players I've known and worked with over the years, Jeff Wilson was special. He was special in so many ways as a rugby player and as a person, but he was special to me personally. Apart from the early years when Jeff was shy and would hardly say boo to a goose, he's been what I call my coalface canary — the bright spot for me when things might get gloomy. I don't know what it was, but he'd always pick my moods and, alone of all the players, he'd do or say something to get me back on an even keel.

"You not happy today Donny? What's the problem?" he'd ask, and I'd know it would be a genuine inquiry, not something that's said for the sake of it. Or he'd ask me if I wasn't feeling well, and he'd take me aside — this boy young enough to be my son! — and ask what he could do to help. After something like this, I'd shake my head, feeling considerably better, and marvel at this boy who was one of rugby's superstars but was taking the time to be concerned about me, a nobody in the great rugby scheme of things.

I probably shouldn't be helping with this little bit of his book because I'm biased. To me, he's not only been one of the greatest rugby players I've seen but a really genuine, caring person. It's a side that the public seldom sees and it's certainly a side the news media doesn't portray, but it's a side I've seen almost daily in all the dealings I've had with him.

I'm happy to help on his book, though, because I consider it a privilege

Flying high in one of the twice-yearly battles between Otago and Southland.

to be asked to do something for Jeff, who I regard as the sort of player who comes along once in a lifetime and whose greatness, perhaps, will only be truly appreciated when it's not on show any more. I'm pretty sure I'll never live to see a player like him again and I count myself lucky that I was around in his era.

I sometimes have wondered whether other players realised just how good he was. When he first came into the Otago team, there had been a lot of publicity about him and some of the more senior Otago players were a bit cynical and skeptical and made unflattering remarks about what "the wonder boy" was going to do.

For the first couple of weeks after he'd arrived in Dunedin, he was ill with food poisoning and didn't take much part in team activities. I'd offer to take him home to his grandmother's house, saying it was on my way (which it wasn't, but he didn't know that) and we'd chat about what he'd done in Invercargill and what he hoped to do now that he was in Otago. He'd get out at his grandmother's and say, "Thanks for the ride, Mr Cameron" and I'd reply, "I'm just Donny, mate." He was such a nice, polite, well brought-up boy.

I remember when the Otago guys first got a sight of what he could do. We were down at the University of Otago gymnasium and Brendon Timmins and Andy Rich and someone else were fooling around with the basketball. As Jeff walked in the door, the ball bounced in his direction and he just grabbed it, spun on a heel and boing! In the basket it went. It must have been from 30 metres away. The others looked and someone said something to the effect of, "Yeah, what a fluke. Bet you can't do that again!" So Jeff got the ball again, went back to the same spot, and did do it again. That was Otago's introduction to the talent of Jeff Wilson, a talent they would see a lot more of, so much that at times they came to rely on it.

Quite often when the team wasn't going well, there'd be almost an unspoken thought in the team that Goldie would get them out of trouble. Give the ball to Jeff, he'll win the game for us. That was the sort of expectation his teammates had of him, so we could only imagine what the expectations were from the public.

We could only imagine, too, the pressure that put on Jeff, though he didn't often show it. He seemed to thrive on it in the early days to such an extent that if he didn't do something wonderful to get his team out of trouble, he'd worry about it and blame himself if Otago lost. That was the sort of thing that happened after the England test in 1993 when Jeff was inconsolable after the game because he blamed himself for the All Blacks losing.

It was only in later years that he matured I suppose and came to appreciate that he couldn't be expected to do everything and therefore didn't try to do everything. He seemed to accept that as long as he did his job as well as he could, that was all that was asked of him. It took longer for other players, and especially critics, to accept that Jeff could not be superman in every game he played. It hurt me when he'd get criticised for his play because even when Jeff had what by his standards was an ordinary game, he was still playing better than most other wings anywhere. His trouble always was that he was judged not by normal standards, but by the much higher ones that he himself had set.

I'm not going to say Jeff is perfect because he's not and he wouldn't thank me for saying he was. He can be withdrawn at times, barely speaking to anyone else, quite content to keep his thoughts to himself and stay with his own company. Sometimes he's been criticised for being moody, but I think it's his way of just taking time out from the constant pressure that's on him to perform. People who have known him well, and that's most of the guys he plays with, know when to involve him and know when just to leave him in peace. I think, and this is entirely understandable, he lives on a different, higher plane to most people because he's so different as an athlete.

He'd be one of the most obstinate, determined people I've ever met. If he decided to do something, or not do something, the most persuasive tongue in the world wouldn't move him from his course. I remember once he had turned an ankle quite badly at training and it swelled up enormously. It was only a couple of days out from an important game and there was no way in the world Jeff was not going to play. "Take a look at it," I said, "it's up like a balloon." "Just rub around it Donny then strap it up, I'm playing." End of conversation.

People watching the Highlanders play the Chiefs at Carisbrook this year may have seen an example of that determination. He twisted an ankle again and after treatment was still hobbling around and Peter Sloane said to get him off before he did any further damage. But Jeff was having none of it. He waved Doc — Steve Bentley, the Highlanders' doctor — away then looked at Sloane in the stand and pointed with both hands to the ground, clearly indicating, "I'm staying!" Sloane bowed to the inevitable.

The thing about Jeff is that he doesn't regard himself as being anything special. He knows he's a gifted athlete of course, but he's a team man first and foremost and he's just one of the boys. You'd never get any airs and graces with him and it makes me wild when I see it written or hear that he's arrogant. Whoever says such a thing has obviously never met him.

If you asked Jeff what he thought of himself, he'd probably say he's just another rugby player, just Joe Bloggs, and I'm sure in his high-pressure sporting life there must have been many times he wished he was just Joe Bloggs.

There are times when Jeff's just a big kid and he's delightful when that happens, which is probably all too rare. They seem to come mostly when the team is doing something different for a change, like a fancy-dress party or something, and it's just the team and partners involved so it's not "the public" Jeff that's being seen. He gets around, entering the spirit of the thing like a giggly kid and it's a wonderful side to see of him. Neither he, nor many other players, get enough such chances to relax and be themselves.

For all the years I've known Jeff, from watching him develop from a talented schoolboy player to one of the best in rugby that I or anyone could have seen, I've always felt that there was an exit door held ready for him to escape through. It wasn't anything he said or did, just a feeling I had that cricket was his escape route from rugby when the pressure got too much, when he wanted a break, or just when he felt he'd done enough.

When he takes that exit, I'll feel privileged that I've been able to see him at his best in a sport that he adorned.

During the Highlanders' bye week in the Super 12 in 1999, the team had an Islanders night. The real one, underneath the wig and false moustache, is Isitolo Maka.

Palenski collection

Tony Gilbert

(Tony Gilbert was assistant coach of Otago for Jeff Wilson's first three years, then coach of the Highlanders and Otago in 1998 and of the Highlanders in 1999. He is now the assistant All Black coach.)

I haven't seen a better player, with the range of skills, the pace and the understanding of the need and the ability to keep the ball alive for his team, than Jeff Wilson. People have called him a once in a lifetime player. He has certainly been the best in my lifetime.

He'll be remembered for his try-scoring skills but there was — is — much more to his play than that. When he wasn't scoring tries, he could do things that other players couldn't conceive of doing. He could take any situation and turn it into something.

I remember once when he'd done a chip and chase try and I remarked to him how impressed I was with his ability to focus on the ball. He replied that he didn't focus on the ball, he focused on the ends of the ball. I was staggered. He had no reason to take the mickey out of me so I could only believe him — that here was a footballer who not only focused on the ball, as every good ball player should, but focused on particular parts of the ball.

I first met Jeff when he was still training to be a teacher and he came as a student teacher to my school, Tahuna Intermediate, to take a science class. I'd heard about him and read about his prodigious sporting feats in Otago and knew I'd be getting to know him better at Carisbrook.

It wasn't just me who had heard of his feats of course and I have a funny feeling when Jeff showed up for his first Otago practice that Stephen Bachop remarked something along the lines of, "Here's the Golden One" or "Here's the Golden Boy", something like that. The "golden" became "Goldie". Jeff's reputation had preceded him and he had to take a fair bit of stick in the dressing room in his early days, as young promising players do from the grizzled old veterans who see the dressing room as their second home. Jeff handled the ribbing without a problem. He was polite, he was focused and he was respectful — he did what he was told when he was told and didn't say much unless he was asked.

He showed from that early age that he had an on-the-ball hunger and skills to match and that's as good as you're going to get.

The try he scored against Auckland in 1993 to win the match, scoring it in the corner in a tackle then converting it from the touchline, was the most emphatic way he could announce his arrival. The next match was Otago's Ranfurly Shield challenge against Waikato and he was left out of the team. He would have been justified in querying the selection, for perhaps being a bit angry about it, but he didn't say a word, just continued to train hard with the reserves and do what was required of him. It was after that shield match that he was named in the All Blacks for the first time.

An aspect of Jeff which doesn't get written about very often is his understanding of the game, his ability to read a game at a level that is beyond most players. I used to say to him that he was sometimes more valuable to us when he didn't have the ball than when he did. His vision on the field was terrific and he could anticipate and move into positions where he would threaten the opposition, without the opposition having a clue about what was coming. He'd see two or three moves ahead and close off a gap that the opposition hadn't yet thought about. That sort of player is worth his weight in gold.

I remember in the Super 12 in 1999 in the round-robin match against the Crusaders that we had a deliberate plan to not let Andrew Mehrtens hit the grass with the ball. If it worked, it would nullify Mehrtens' tactical game and eventually put him off. All the onus was on Jeff to anticipate what Mehrtens was going to do and be in position to take the ball. Mehrtens is a very smart player. Jeff proved to be smarter and followed the plan to the letter. The Crusaders didn't score a try that day and, by halftime, Merhtens' game had fallen off.

Another Wilson strength was the energy he brought to his play. He had this powerful energy around the ball and an ability to be fully engaged in some difficult manoeuvre while at the same time being able to plan what would happen next and then what would happen after that.

A player such as Wilson also lifted everyone around him. While he was performing his wondrous deeds, his teammates would lift their games and their concentration, knowing they were in the presence of greatness and dare not let it down. This was also evident at trainings and I remember when he was passed fit to play after missing the first few games of the Super 12 in 1998. The doctor showed up at training, examined Jeff's hand, said he probably couldn't aggravate the injury and asked him if he wanted to play in the next match. Jeff's eyes lit up and he raced back to the rest of the backs, telling them he was in. The lift in training from then was immediately noticeable.

I was saddened, but not all that surprised, when I was told Jeff would not be available for the All Blacks in 2000. I'd got a feeling for what he was going through and it was obvious to Wayne Smith and me that he was not enjoying his rugby as much as he had. We still would have picked him, though, there's no doubt about that. Such class and talent is not dismissed lightly.

I was looking forward to the special qualities he would bring to the All Blacks — and I hope that I can still look forward to that. There is something

Against the Auckland Blues in 1999, a rare win for an Otago team over an Auckland team.

about him and his understanding of the game that puts him several levels ahead of most players, and of some coaches. He must have been frustrated at times, knowing what he wanted a team to do but also knowing that the other players were not of that level, either in terms of thought or of action.

I hope the All Blacks haven't seen the last of him. For all he's achieved, there is still much promise there. Perhaps he could come back in a different position, and there are two that I'd love to see him in. I think that with his vision, understanding and skills, he'd make a wonderful centre. I watched him play a couple of games at centre for his Dunedin club, Harbour, and the two things that struck me were the time he had — a hallmark of greatness — and the fact the wings scored all the tries.

The other position is first five-eighth, where he played at school for a time and only occasionally since. I believe he would be as successful at first five-eighth as he has been on the wing or at fullback. He's got everything a great first five-eighth needs.

That's the word that really sums Wilson up: great.

14. What now?

Photosport

For the first time for more years than I can remember, I've had some time to myself, time in which I haven't been thinking about a game, practising for a game, playing a game, recovering from a game, or thinking about the next one.

I don't want to sound as if I'm wallowing in self-pity because I'm not; I've enjoyed my life and particularly my sport and I'm grateful for the opportunities and honours that have come my way. But I feel as if I have missed some growing up along the way, as if sporting years merged into one another and crowded out the normal things in life that other people do. I

When the All Blacks got under way in 2000, I was learning how the other half lived. At North Harbour Stadium in Albany for the test against Tonga.

seemed to have gone straight from school into the New Zealand cricket team and into the All Blacks and had been on the sporting rollercoaster ever since.

It was time to get off.

The catalyst, as I explained publicly in May when I said I was taking time out from rugby, was the death of my father Bill late in 1998. His death was a shattering blow to me, as the loss of a father must be to any son. All sons must, or at least should, think of their fathers as special people and Bill was certainly special to me and to my brother Richard. Whatever I did in sport, whether it was rugby or cricket, it was in partnership with Bill. I was out there in the middle doing it, but I was an extension of him. We built a sporting career together, he and I, and then, for the first time in my life, I was left on my own.

It was a different Jeff Wilson who played the Super 12, the domestic tests, the tri-nations and the World Cup in 1999 and, as the months unfolded, I came to realise how different. I tried not to think that Dad wasn't in the stand watching, or wasn't sitting at home watching on television, ready to tell me afterwards what I'd done wrong and what I may have done right. I tried not to think of the absence but it was there in my subconscious all the time.

I seemed to play through 1999 partly in a vacuum, partly from memory, and partly in memory of my father. I could still do things on the rugby field that I'd always done, I was still absolutely committed to the teams I played for, and I was still terribly proud to be playing for my country, but something was missing. My alter ego, my father, was missing, and as a result I gradually lost the desire.

I first started thinking about retirement, or at least not playing for a while, after the All Blacks lost the World Cup semifinal to France. It wasn't because we lost the match, it was because we lost the chance to win the World Cup and the four-year cycle would begin again. I said to reporters at the time that I didn't think I'd be around for the next World Cup but neither they nor I really knew when my departure would come. But come it assuredly would.

John Hart and I had always got on well and I first broached the subject with him when we were in Cardiff for the playoff match against South Africa. I told him everything there was to know and, like a good listener, he listened, not attempting to persuade me into any particular course of action but saying I would have his support whatever I chose to do and that genuine rugby people would understand.

All Blacks, and rugby players generally, often say that the end of a tour is the worst time to consider the future. At that stage, bodies are tired and minds are jaded and there's a risk that a decision could be made that would later be regretted. The time to decide on hanging up the boots, to use the time-honoured rugby phrase, is after a summer, after a rest, and when it's time to start thinking about getting back into training again. The trouble with rugby these days is that there is precious little time between one season and another, especially if the All Blacks have been to the northern hemisphere. Finish there in November or even December, then back into Super 12 training in January. It is insufficient time away from a game with such a degree of physical contact.

My rest after the World Cup was doing the European tour with my mother, having just a day or two in London with friends, and a bit more time with friends in Fiji on the way home. It was a time for thinking.

When I was back in New Zealand, Peter Sloane was appointed coach of the Highlanders to take over from Tony Gilbert and I was sufficiently encouraged by that to decide to carry on for at least the Super 12, to see how I felt, to see if the spark was back. Sloane being the coach gave me heart that it would be a happy team, that we'd play with a whole team concept with the idea of making the ball do all the work. That was my kind of rugby.

But the spark wasn't back. I was jaded. Though the death of my father was a big factor, it wasn't the only one. I needed a break. I was only 26 years old but had played nearly 200 games of first-class rugby. I was playing something like 30 games a year, none at a lower standard than playing for Otago, whereas when I began I'd played only six or seven perhaps in a year. In my first year of first-class rugby, in 1992, I played just seven games. In my second year, in 1993, I played 21 games, even with an All Black tour thrown in. By the end of the 90s, it was at least 30 games a year.

When it's considered that most of those games, 90 per cent of them, are either tests or Super 12 matches or games in which there is an expectation of a high-calibre performance, it can be very draining, physically and mentally. I know tennis players and golfers and baseballers and soccer players and racing drivers all have long seasons, and maybe others from other sports too, but none I suggest involves the physical impact that rugby has. Players of the past used to say it would take them a fortnight to recover mentally and physically from a test, and they'd play only five or six a year, with no Super 12 and, before 1976, no NPC either with the week in and week out quest for competition points.

Some players can and do thrive on such a heavy workload, but some players do not. My attitude to sport is to give everything you've got when you're playing, to not hold back in what might be deemed a lesser game. I'd like to think my attitude to playing a club game for Harbour in Dunedin, something I sadly didn't do as often as I would have liked, was just the same as my attitude to playing a test. Games are there to be won and I'm there to do my best for my team, whatever it takes.

I found in 1999 and early in 2000 that I was playing too much for someone with my attitude toward sport. I had difficulty "getting up" for games, and I wasn't enjoying the training any more. I remember once after an early-season training with the Highlanders I went and slumped in the gear room afterward and pulled a Speight's out of the refrigerator. That was something I had never done before, and not something I've done since either. But it was a small measure of how I was feeling toward the physical side of rugby.

My enthusiasm for the game and for being with my teammates had not waned at all. I love rugby and I love being around teammates, especially the Highlanders or Otago. The Highlanders this year were a great bunch of guys and I thoroughly enjoyed their company. What I didn't enjoy was the training and the playing and, for someone used to 100 per cent commitment, that was untenable.

Halfway through the Super 12, I went and saw Peter Sloane and told him that I couldn't continue. My heart was with the Highlanders, but my head wasn't. I was still trying to do my best, but there's no substitute for desire, and that was what was missing. Sloaney and I had a good chat about it, in much the same way as John Hart and I had in Cardiff, and he made it clear to me that he would support me whatever I did. I decided to carry on for the sake of the team, not to leave them midstream, not to let them down.

I know that my rugby wasn't of the standard I normally expect of myself. I know I made uncharacteristic mistakes, either of execution or in deciding options, and they were an indication of the way I was feeling. It was not nice to be told that I was being criticised on talkback radio — no matter who delivers uninformed opinions, no one likes being criticised — and neither was it any consolation to be told that even in the ordinary form that I was in, I was still among the best wings in the country. Playing against the Brumbies in Canberra, I missed a fairly straightforward tackle on Andrew Walker, who went on to score one of his umpteen tries, and of course everyone in the world noticed that. That hurt.

The Highlanders' last three round-robin matches in the Super 12 were in South Africa and Australia and I told two or three people before we left that I would not be continuing after the Super 12. They didn't try to dissuade me though I could see in their eyes that they wished I was continuing. But I'd made up my mind. I couldn't continue in that frame of mind. I wasn't doing justice to myself, my teammates, the people who trusted me, and I wasn't doing justice to the memory of my father.

It was time to go. I wasn't prepared to be just an ordinary rugby player. It wasn't because I was getting older, not because I was losing skills or anything like that. The desire just wasn't there.

I played one more game on Carisbrook, against the Chiefs, and as luck would have it twisted an ankle and ordinarily would have followed the advice of our doctor, Steve Bentley, and left the field. But I told him I was staying on. He said something to Peter Sloane in the stand and Sloaney indicated I should be replaced. I dug my heels in. Well, one good heel anyway.

I looked up at Sloaney and pointed to the ground in a gesture that said plainly, "I'm staying". I didn't want to finish what may have been my last game on Carisbrook as a replaced cripple on the bench.

When we were in Sydney for the last match before the semifinal, David Howman came from Wellington to see me. He told me he'd already spoken to David Rutherford, the chief executive of the New Zealand union, and that he also supported me in my decision.

I was encouraged by the backing I received from the New Zealand and Otago unions, each of which I was still contracted to. I'd told my old basketball coach and close friend, Tab Baldwin, and I'd told some of the players when we were in South Africa; Anton Oliver was clever enough to guess what was happening and I told Josh Kronfeld the day before the semifinal in Christchurch. That was why he came to me at the end of the game and embraced me, with him saying, "You're going before me, you bastard!" I told the rest of the Highlanders squad at a team meeting in Christchurch after the game, then made it public the next morning.

The end of the road – temporarily anyway. Josh and I embrace after the Super 12 semifinal in Christchurch.

Peter Bush

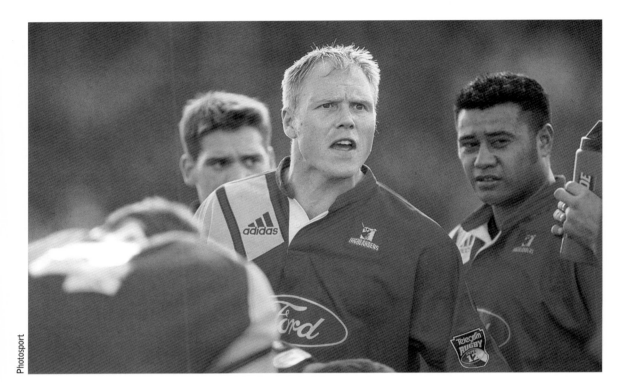

Making a point during what turned out to be the last match – for a while, anyway.

It was a relief that it was done, but there was a tinge of sadness too.

It was time to move on; there were things to do, a life to live, new things to discover. I'd see my family, see friends I hadn't been able to see for years, drive around a bit, do things I couldn't do as a rugby player. In short, I'd lead a life of normality and some stability. I'd had a house built on the edge of the Taieri Plains south of Dunedin and was looking forward to settling in there. I keep my private life to myself as much as possible but, in a place like Dunedin, word doesn't take long to get around and an amazing number of people seemed to find the need to drive down my relatively obscure road and almost stall outside my house. Part of the price, I guess.

The break gave me an opportunity to get my body right. I'd had niggling shoulder and ankle injuries and with the constant diet of train and play, there's never the chance to completely rehabilitate from such injuries. So the first thing I did was to get myself right, to get myself fully fit and be in the best shape of my entire life. That was a challenge for me alone — for the first time, it was not a challenge for me and Dad. It was something I would have to do myself without my father's strength behind me. That was what I was coming to terms with. Everything I'd done in sport had been in tandem with Dad. Now, I'm making the decisions on my own and I felt I needed to be able to do that and time away from the pressures of playing allowed that to happen.

I now had to answer solely to myself, no one else. There was no question that I wanted to continue to play sport, either rugby or cricket, maybe both, maybe something else, and it was a matter of getting the body right and deciding when the desire had returned. I had no intention of getting back into sport without being fully committed. That's not the way I do things. The only difference was that this time I was doing it on my own, and I needed time to adjust to doing things that way.

I was heartened by the support I had from people close to me and from people who didn't know me at all, but thought they did from years of watching me on television. Any criticism of me wouldn't have worried me in the slightest because such criticism would have been based on just the flimsiest grasp of the facts and could therefore be dismissed. But there wasn't even much of that. I felt that in making the decision public the way I did, I was being honest with everyone but, most importantly, I was being honest with myself.

I left, if only temporarily, a game that I love but a game for which I had some worries. For the first time, I was able to listen to the announcement of the All Black squad at the end of May knowing that there was no chance my name would be in it. I could look from the outside with a sense of detachment, understanding what was going on but not being a part of it.

Book publishing deadlines being what they are, this was written before the All Blacks had played in 2000 and I was as interested as anyone to see how they fared and to see how the two coaches, Wayne Smith and Tony Gilbert, coped with all the pressures that being with the All Blacks bring. By the end of the year, they would understand better — and perhaps the public would too — the pressures that the team and in particular John Hart were under in 1999. The All Blacks' results would also allow a more accurate measure of the 1999 team. There's nothing like a bit of time to add perspective and if there was one thing the reaction to the World Cup results needed, it was perspective. We've seen it since with the emotive response to Russell Coutts and Brad Butterworth deciding to ply their yachting trade away from New Zealand.

It's often intrigued me that those who aspire to success, especially sporting success, are most often vilified by people with no aspirations of their own.

Rugby to me is the ultimate of team games — cricket is more a game played by individuals for a team — and it saddened me a little to see, and be a part of, individuals in rugby being placed higher than the team. This happened to me, especially in my younger days, and it happened also to players such as Jonah Lomu (to a much greater degree), Christian Cullen and Sean Fitzpatrick. The marketing of rugby and the media — in the widest possible sense, including advertising agencies — built up individuals far too much, though they did it brilliantly I might add. Television commercials and

Wilson collection

**Away from rugby,
I could take a greater
interest in netball ...
and Adine Harper.**

promotional campaigns push individuals rather than the team as a whole and I don't think that's healthy for the essential ethos of rugby. In a team, we're all interdependent and that's the way it should be, not one or two above others. This was particularly noticeable in 1999 with the adidas advertisements and a couple of commercials. It may be the way it's done in Europe, but it's not the way it should be done in New Zealand and one of the reasons the All Blacks have been historically so successful is that they have always been the complete team in all things.

That's why I like the advertising campaigns run in Otago. It's all focused on the team, not on Jeff Wilson or Josh Kronfeld or Taine Randell or whoever, and that's the way it should be. For adidas and others who seek to promote the All Blacks, the lesson is that bigger is not necessarily better. Making us out to be larger than life is ultimately counter-productive.

I have concerns about the way the game is going and there were times in the Super 12 in 2000 that I felt I was playing some sort of glorified rugby league; players lined out laterally across the field with all the emphasis on defence. And for those sensitive souls who follow league, this is not a criticism of their sport. If people want to play league, fine. But don't confuse the two. I played rugby because it was rugby, but the rugby I played in 2000 was vastly different from the rugby I played in 1993.

The laws are such now that they are weighted in favour of the team with possession with the result that the first aim is ball retention and the second is defence. The Brumbies, much smarter than New Zealand teams, are masters at this new form of rugby but the Crusaders aren't far behind, especially when they can use someone with the intelligence of Andrew Mehrtens.

The net result is that the team that makes fewer mistakes will almost invariably win and that the rewards for enterprising, exciting rugby are fast disappearing. Restarts have become the most important part of the game because that is when possession is decided and, once gained, a team with the ball will dominate. There are fewer genuine contests for possession so that one team has the ball and the other defends. This then has the effect of whittling away at the physical and mental strength of the defending team. It's a fact that the more tackles you make, the more tired you are and that when you may eventually get the ball, you're so tired you've barely got the energy to do much with it, or even to think about what to do with it.

I think it's sad that that's where the game has gone. Rugby in essence is a simple game but it's been made complicated by the proliferation of laws and the varied interpretation of those laws. The tackle ball law especially, though

**Boys and their toys ...
me and my Mustang**

Studio Microdot

better than it was, is still a minefield of confusion and opinion. We can do one thing quite legitimately in one game, then get penalised mercilessly in the next for the same thing. Confused players don't make for good players, and a confused public will just find something else to watch.

There need to be more contests for possession, especially at lineouts, while offside laws need to be rigidly policed, especially in the backs. There's nothing worse for attacking back play than to have the opposition backs up in your face at the same time as you receive the ball. It may be time for rugby touch judges, soccer-style, to start signalling offsides and forward passes.

Rugby is going through a phase, as it has many times before. The laws will change, a new style will evolve, smart coaches or players — probably Australians! — will find ways of exploiting or avoiding the new laws. New strategies will evolve, new stars will emerge.

Such is rugby. It has faults, but it's a game I love and it's a game that has given me moments and memories that I will treasure. I hope that I've been able to give some in return.

Afterword

It is the end of the golden weather. That was a lovely, uniquely New Zealand phrase by Bruce Mason. In allusion and in fact, it fits neatly as a description of the temporary departure of Jeff Wilson, unique also in his way.

All sports people must retire at some stage. Some choose their method of going, some have the choice taken from them; some stay on as long as they can, others quit before the writing appears on the wall. Some go before what is popularly seen as their time. Two athletes from two entirely different sports of an earlier time, Ron Jarden and Peter Snell, come to mind. Both retired at what was seen as an early age, when the public perception was that they still had fields to conquer, races to run. We saw the best of them, of that there was no doubt, but we the selfish public wanted to see more of the best of them.

So with Jeffrey William Wilson. We have seen the best. We have seen a supreme competitor and a multi-skilled practitioner at his best in two sports, but especially in rugby. There was a sense, as he was in what was best termed a time out from the game, a feeling of being cheated, of being deprived. We had seen the best, yes, but there was still some best yet to see.

There is an adage in show business that the time to leave the stage is when the audience is crying for more; leave them at their peak, not at their trough. Go when the praise is highest, don't wait for the time — more inevitable in sport than it is in show business — when the praise will wane.

Wilson chose to step away for a number of reasons, mainly because he wanted, as he put it, time to himself, time to consider not just what he would do for the rest of his life, but to consider life itself.

That has to be placed in its proper context of this extraordinary sporting individual. Since he was a young teenager in Invercargill, he had been lionised and fêted as a sporting prodigy, someone who would be an outstanding success at whichever sport he turned his hand to. Cricket, rugby, basketball, athletics — all were available to him, and him to them.

This is not the time nor place to speculate on what he may have achieved in other sports, nor to speculate on what he may yet do, but to reflect on what he did achieve in the two for which he was most noted: rugby and

cricket, and for us the public to feel privileged that we lived in the same age as he and that we were able to bear witness to his greatness.

That is not to place either him or sport too highly in the human order of things. It is entirely human for someone to wish they'd seen something they didn't, but have only read or heard about. There must be rugby followers who have heard all about Bert Cooke, the prince of the midfield of the 20s, and wished they could have seen him, so they could have seen for themselves the manner of his genius. Equally, there must be others who wished they'd seen Jack Lovelock run, Anthony Wilding play tennis, Yvette Williams compete in the long jump or any of the other events that she graced.

It is, after all, why we go to sports events; for the immediacy as well as for the afterglow. In sport, as the years condemn and at the going down of our own sun, there is no prouder boast than to say "I was there . . ." or "I saw . . ."

So we saw "Goldie", a name he once tolerated rather than liked, but which he felt he grew out of. We saw him as a teenager, doing in reality what other teenagers do in their dreams, scoring the winning runs for New Zealand, scoring tries for the All Blacks, kicking goals, making crucial defensive tackles. We saw him at times take personal hold of matches, an individual controlling the destiny of a game of rugby, the ultimate of team games; we saw him do with seeming nonchalant ease what other, lesser players make look difficult because it is difficult; we saw the arcing, gliding runs, the defence unsure whether Wilson was going to beat them on the outside or on the inside because he could do both, and beat them he assuredly would. We saw the perfection of the chip and chase, and the exultation of a good team try scored, the arms raised to the crowds, either mocking them or encouraging them, depending on the allegiance of the crowd in the immediate vicinity.

We saw a player who, in rugby, spanned the amateur and the professional eras and was comfortable with both; a youth for whom the ultimate honour was to play for his country and it was irrelevant whether he was paid for it or not and a man who was paid for it but still carried with him the youthful zest and pride of pulling on the All Black jersey. Players don't call it the All Black jersey. It is The Jersey. Wilson was such a proud All Black he pronounced the capitals.

We saw also, in that transient amateur-to-professional phase, a young man wooed by the sirens of unimaginable money, but then not yielding to the temptation, staying loyal instead to all that he and New Zealand held dear. He was rewarded handsomely of course for his loyalty, but New Zealand rugby and New Zealand generally benefited as well.

If we were privileged to see Wilson, and we were, we were even more privileged to see in the same team and at the same time two other players,

Jeff Wilson set to beat Russell Bennett in the All Blacks' big win against South Africa at Eden Park in 1997.

Jonah Lomu and Christian Cullen, who had their own once-in-a-lifetime status. Can any All Black team have had such riches to call on at the one time, can any followers have been so fortunate to have seen three such players on the same afternoon (or night)?

It makes it even more of an oddity that an All Black team with Wilson, and with Cullen on one occasion and Lomu on two, could not win rugby's ultimate prize, the World Cup. There were reasons why this was sadly so, some attributable to the caprices of sporting fates, and some attributable to reasons which will remain speculative.

But it is a fact, and possibly will remain so, that for all the Wilson genius, for all the talent that surrounded him, the one major rugby trophy he was able to savour and hold aloft was the NPC trophy when his beloved Otago won in 1998. No World Cup, no Ranfurly Shield. It is a Wilson CV that seems somehow incomplete. How can such sustained brilliance be so cruelly rewarded? Well, as Wilson might say, that's the way it goes sometimes.

In any sporting life, there are turning points, some noticeable at the time, some apparent only because of the beneficial wisdom of hindsight. A turning point in the career of Jeff Wilson was not long after the Otago NPC win in 1998 when his father, Bill, died unexpectedly. It is always a sad blow for a son when he loses a father. For Wilson, it had an impact beyond the personal loss. His closest friend and advisor, his business manager and the man who understood him best and to whom he responded best, was not there any more. Others tried to breach the gap, but it was unbreachable.

Wilson could still do things on a rugby field that others could not or did not; he could still in the twinkling of an eye turn a match with a piece of audacious and inspired brilliance, but the joy and the zest for the game were not as evident as they had been before.

There were other reasons, as there will always be in a team game, in a game in which success is utterly dependent on each member of the team doing his designated job accurately, time and again, and in which the opponents try to deter such commitment to a cause.

But the impression grew in 1999 and early in 2000 that this was a different Wilson we were seeing. He was still gifted, still supremely fit, still dedicated, but the heart didn't seem in it as much as previously.

Bill Wilson's death was not the only factor, but the main one. Jeff Wilson had been playing rugby at the highest level, year in and year out, since 1993. His life, off the field and on, was consumed by rugby, relegating everything else, including the cricket he so much enjoys, to a casual status that could be fitted in when there was time, of which there was never enough.

This combination of factors led to the decision to leave rugby, at least for a time. When he first made it known, there were those who couldn't believe it and there were those who sought to dissuade him. But the Wilson mind was made up and he brings to his decision-making the same dogged determination he brings to his sporting pursuits.

So where, when Wilson entered the ranks of "former All Black", perhaps temporarily, did that leave us? It left us the appetising prospect of a possible return to cricket, it left us tantalisingly wondering if we'll see him as an All Black again, and it left us with a legacy that anyone would be proud to leave. Whatever else Jeff Wilson does in his life, whether it's in sport or anything else, he's already given us enough good memories to be going on with.

Ron Palenski, Dunedin, 2000

Wellington coach Frank Walker said after Otago's 32-27 win against Wellington in the NPC in 1997: "The magic of Jeff Wilson was too much for us." Wilson confronts fullback Jeremy Coulter.

Statistics

- His 209 points for the All Blacks in tests put him third on the all-time list behind Grant Fox and Andrew Mehrtens.

- His 39 tries in tests were a record, four ahead of John Kirwan.

- His 41 tests in succession (1996-99) were the third most behind Sean Fitzpatrick (63) and Robin Brooke (49).

- His five tries against Fiji in 1997 were the second-most in a test (after Marc Ellis's seven).

- He is second on the All Blacks' World Cup try-scoring list with nine, six behind Jonah Lomu.

- By the end of 1999, Wilson's 16 tri-nations tests gave him a share of the record with Christian Cullen, Robin Brooke and Justin Marshall.

- His 65 matches for New Zealand are a record for an Otago player (beating Kevin Skinner's 61).

Jeff Wilson in rugby
(to 1 June, 2000)

Team	Year	Matches	Tests	Tries	Conversions	Penalty goals	Dropped goals	Total points
New Zealand	1993	9	2	6	5	6	-	58
	1994	1	1	-	-	-	-	-
	1995	12	10	7	4	2	-	49
	1996	10	10	5	-	-	-	25
	1997	13	12	12	2	-	-	64
	1998	7	7	4	-	-	-	20
	1999	13	12	11	-	-	1	58
	Totals	65	54	45	11	8	1	274
Southland	1992	7		4	-	-	-	20
	Totals	7		4				20
Otago	1993	11		3	21	19	-	114
	1994	9		5	14	14	-	95
	1995	15		9	11	11	3	109
	1996	6		5	-	-	-	25
	1997	7		5	-	-	-	25
	1998	8		8	1	-	-	42
	Totals	56		35	47	44	3	410
Highlanders	1996	11		6	8	8	-	70
	1997	8		4	-	-	-	20
	1998	9		10	-	-	-	50
	1999	12		2	1	-	-	12
	2000	12		5	-	1	-	28
	Totals	52		27	9	9	-	180
NZ trials	1993	1		-	-	-	-	-
	1994	1		-	-	-	-	-
	1995	1		1	-	-	-	5
NZ Colts	1993	2		4	5	3	-	39
Divisional XV	1993	1		-	-	-	-	-
New Zealand XV	1994	1		-	-	-	-	
NZ Development	1994	6		7	1	-	-	37
South Island	1995	1		1	-	4	-	17
Harlequins	1995	1		2	-	-	-	10
President's XV	1996	1		3	-	-	-	15
Barbarians	1997-8	2		2	-	-	-	10
Rugby Academy	1997	1		5	1	-	-	27
	Totals	19		25	7	7		160

Keeping myself, and a photographer, amused when in Sydney for the 1999 Bledisloe Cup test.

Total first-class

Matches	Tries	Conversions	Penalties	Dropped goals	Total points
199	136	74	68	4	1044

Tries in tests

Tries	Against	Venue	Year
1, 2, 3	Scotland	Edinburgh	1993
4	Canada	Auckland	1995
5, 6, 7	Japan	Bloemfontein	1995
8	Australia	Sydney	1995
9	Italy	Bologna	1995
10	Western Samoa	Napier	1996
11	Australia	Wellington	1996
12	South Africa	Durban	1996
13, 14	South Africa	Pretoria	1996
15, 16, 17, 18, 19	Fiji	Albany	1997
20	South Africa	Johannesburg	1997
21	Australia	Melbourne	1997
22, 23	Ireland	Dublin	1997
24	England	Manchester	1997
25, 26	England	Dunedin	1998
27, 28	England	Auckland	1998
29, 30, 31, 32	Samoa	Albany	1999
33	South Africa	Dunedin	1999
34	England	London	1999
35, 36, 37	Italy	Huddersfield	1999
38	Scotland	Edinburgh	1999
39	France	London	1999

One of two tries against England at Eden Park in 1998.

Photosport

Batting										Bowling					
M	Inn	NO	HS	Runs	Ave	100	50	Ct	St	W	Runs	Ave	5wi	10wm	Best
24	45	4	78	845	20.60	-	4	21	-	86	1925	22.38	4	-	5-48

One-day internationals

Batting							Bowling				
M	Inn	NO	HS	Runs	Ave	Ct	Balls	Runs	Wkts	Ave	Best
4	4	1	44*	80	26.66	1	152	135	3	45.00	2-21

Double All Blacks

	RUGBY		CRICKET	
	Tests	Others	Tests	Others*
George Dickinson	1922		1924-25, 1931-32	
	-	5	3	3
Charlie Oliver	1928, 29, 34-36		1925-26, 27	
	7	26	-	15
Curly Page	1928		1926-27—1937-38	
	-	1	14	72
Eric Tindill	1935, 36, 38		1936-37, 1946-47	
	1	16	5	24
Bill Carson	1938		1937, 38, 39	
	-	3	-	22
Brian McKechnie	1977-79, 81		1975—1980-81	
	10	16	-	16
Jeff Wilson	1993-2000		1993	
	54	11	-	4

* comprises first-class matches and one-day internationals

Howzat? Surely, he must have been out. Against Australia in 1993.

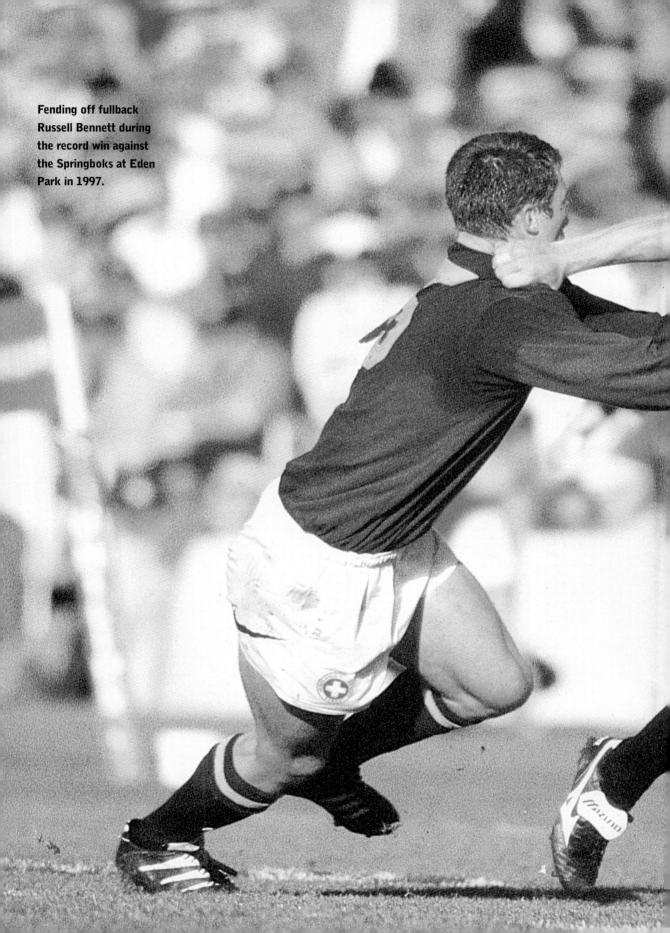

Fending off fullback
Russell Bennett during
the record win against
the Springboks at Eden
Park in 1997.